On the Trail of Flora Thompson

Flora Jane Thompson was born (neé Timms) in 1876 at Juniper Hill on the Oxfordshire/Northamptonshire border. She started work in a neighbouring post office at the age of fourteen, thus beginning a long connection with the Post Office. At the age of twenty-one, she took a position as sub-office assistant to the postmaster in Grayshott, Hampshire, and was to stay in Hampshire, more or less, for the next thirty years of her life. On leaving Grayshott she moved to Bournemouth and in January 1903 married John Thompson. Their daughter Winifred (called Diana) was born in October of that year, and their first son Basil in 1909. In 1916, a month after Flora's favourite brother Edwin was killed in action in Belgium, John Thompson applied for the position of postmaster at Liphook.

The family thus moved back to within three miles of Grayshott, and Flora was able to renew her acquaintance with the area. Easier times followed the end of the First World War and, despite the arrival of a third child, Peter, in 1918, Flora began writing more industriously during this period than at any other time. Here she wrote her nature notes, *The Peverel Papers*, from her own observations during her long and frequent walks in the area, and here in 1926 the family bought a house of their own for the first time, having previously been forced to live in rented Post Office accommodation. But hardly had they settled in than John Thompson applied for promotion again, and moved to Dartmouth in November 1927. Flora stayed in her beloved Liphook for nearly a year more while the house was sold, and then followed, never to return to Hampshire.

During the next ten years she revised some of the notes she had written about her early childhood and developed them into the book *Lark Rise* which was to bring her fame late in life. The success of this book led to the publication of two more, and their eventual appearance as the trilogy *Lark Rise to Candleford*. She wrote a fourth book, *Heatherley*, a sequel following on from *Candleford Green* and telling of her time in Grayshott, but chose not to publish it. Instead, she wrote *Still Glides the Stream* — her final publication.

Flora Thompson died at Brixham, Devon, on 21st May 1947.

Sketch showing Flora as she describes herself arriving in Grayshott, September 1898 — Hester Whittle

On the Trail
of
Flora Thompson

ରୀ ରୀ ରୀ

Heatherley to Peverel

Grayshott to Griggs Green

On the Trail of Flora Thompson
First published 1997
Reprinted 1998

Typeset and published by John Owen Smith
12 Hillside Close, Headley Down, Hampshire GU35 8BL

Tel/Fax: 01428 712892
E-mail: wordsmith@headley1.demon.co.uk
Web site: www.headley1.demon.co.uk

ISBN 1-873855-24-9

Printed and bound by Antony Rowe Ltd, Bumper's Farm, Chippenham, Wiltshire

Contents

*Flora in her early
twenties*

Illustrations

☙☙☙

Illustrations (contd)

Illustrations acknowledgements:—

Roger Blake–2, 7; Eileen Chapman & Isobel A'Court–3, 4;
Laurence Giles–17,18,23,29,33; Richard Hawkes–11;
David Lindsay–28; Gillian Lindsay–27; Mrs Irene Lorimer–20;
Mrs Audrey Mylne–15; Peter Sillick–14; Mrs Vivienne Stubbs–21;
Mrs Fiona White–31; Hester Whittle–cover sketch of Flora;
Tim Winter–9; BT Archives Photographic Library–6;
British Newspaper Library–24, 25, 26; Cable & Wireless plc–15;
National Archives of Canada–22; Hampshire Record Office–M4;
Haslemere Museum–10, 19; The Herald Group of Newspapers–8;
Oxfordshire Photographic Archive–5; Surrey Local Studies Library,
Guildford–M1, M2.

Other illustrations – the author.

Author's Note

In setting out *On the Trail of Flora Thompson*, I have used as my prime sources her published works connected with east Hampshire; these being *A Country Calendar and other writings* selected and edited by Margaret Lane and published by Oxford University Press in 1979, and extracts from *The Peverel Papers* selected by Julian Shuckburgh and published in 1986 by Century Hutchinson Ltd. Other published sources used include: the book called *Grayshott* published by the late J. H. (Jack) Smith in 1978; the various historical booklets published over several years by the Bramshott & Liphook Preservation Society; the 1990 biography *Flora Thompson* by Gillian Lindsay; and *The Hilltop Writers* published by W. R. (Bob) Trotter in 1996.

But, naturally enough, the most exciting sources were the unexpected and unpublished ones, those that came from ferreting through various public and private archives, hunting for clues, tracking down descendants and others who might have anything to add to the story; writing, phoning, visiting, recording, and finally piecing the jigsaw puzzle together.

The process was enjoyable, and in so many interesting ways the story which emerged was not entirely the one as told by Flora.

Flora's granddaughter, Mrs Elizabeth Swaffield, has kindly allowed me to publish in full the missing chapter of *Heatherley* and other related information which Gillian Lindsay discovered in the archives of the Harry Ransom Humanities Research Center at the University of Texas. The Center also has given permission for me to use the material, and naturally I extend my thanks to Gillian for her readiness to pass on the information to me in the first place.

I acknowledge the kind permission of Oxford University Press in allowing me to quote from *A Country Calendar*. Where I have done this, the text is set within single quotation marks—as also where I have quoted directly from other sources.

Flora's pseudonyms for people and places are also set within single quotation marks, except where they occur within already quoted passages. Note in particular that, continuing the style she adopted in *Lark Rise*, Flora referred to herself throughout *Heatherley* in the third-person, as 'Laura'.

I should like to thank the many people who have given me help and encouragement along the way. To try to name them all would require a feat of memory beyond my means. Some, such as Anne Mallinson and Gillian Lindsay, I have mentioned elsewhere in the context of their particular kindness, but I must make special reference here to the following who helped me with family reminiscences or eye-witness accounts relating to the Thompsons:—

> Isabel A'Court, Eileen Chapman and the late Ray Chapman, children of Annie Symonds;
> Phyllis Beard, sister of Cecil Cluer;
> Irene Lorimer, daughter of 'Louie' Woods;
> Joe Leggett and his sister Eileen Hobson, who were next-door neighbours of the Thompsons at Griggs Green;
> Audrey Mylne, grandniece of William Elwes.

And no work relating to the history of the Liphook district would be complete without expressing my sincere thanks to Laurence Giles and the Bramshott & Liphook Preservation Society for their efforts in recording the past events and personalities of their parish in such an accessible form. As an 'interloper' from a neighbouring parish, I hope I have been able to repay their kindness a little in producing this book to add to their store.

John Owen Smith
Headley 1997

Introduction

❦ ❦ ❦

Beyond Candleford Green

Flora Thompson wrote a minor classic in the last years of her life, describing evocatively her childhood days in north Oxfordshire during the 1880s and 1890s. Her three books, best known now in their trilogy form as *Lark Rise to Candleford*, give a unique and personal view of a cottage child growing up at a time when 'many of the old village ways of living still remained, and those who cherished the old customs were much as country people had been for generations.'

But these works were not completed until she was over sixty years old. She had been 'a great spoiler of paper,' to use her own words, for as long as she could remember, but public acclaim late in her life came only after many years of less successful authorship—years during which she left her Oxfordshire roots and moved to other parts of the country.

Starting work, she tells us, as a 'learner' in the 'Candleford Green' post office at the age of fourteen, still within walking distance of her home, Flora gained enough confidence over the next six years to think about looking for a job further afield. At the age of twenty she took 'an opportunity,' and 'driven on by well-meant advice from without, and from within by the restless longing of youth to see and experience the whole of life, she disappeared from the country scene,' as she puts it.

Then we lose track of her for about a year. She tells us she took 'short holiday-relief engagements' at various post offices, and that her people at home began to speak of her as a 'rolling stone.' We also know that at least part of this 'lost' year was spent in Essex, but in September 1898 we find her taking a position which she hoped would become a 'permanency,' as sub office assistant to the postmaster in the Hampshire village of Grayshott.

And having arrived there, she fell in love immediately with the heather-clad landscape. 'Dear, warm, tender Hampshire,' she wrote later. 'Very few have praised her, yet she is most

11

worthy; a dark Madonna, with heather-purple robe and deep pine tresses, sitting in the sun with a blessing for all who seek her.' It was, she tells us, a 'falling in love' on her part with those aspects of the county which she found so different from her native soil— the sharp tang of pine trees, hilltop views and endless carpets of purple heather contrasting with the heavy, earthy scents and flat cornfields of her youth.

She was to continue this love affair with heathland Hampshire for the next thirty years or so. In 1900/1901 she moved from Grayshott, married another post office worker and settled in Bournemouth near to the New Forest. Then in August 1916 her husband was appointed postmaster at Liphook, just three miles from Grayshott, and she was able to reacquaint herself with the area. She finally left the county in the autumn of 1928 to follow, reluctantly, another career move of her husband's—this time to Dartmouth in Devon.

It was during her time in Hampshire, however, that she matured, married and became a mother—also the time during which she began seriously to practice the craft of writing. While living in Liphook she had her first book published, a slim volume of poetry entitled *Bog Myrtle and Peat*, and here also she started to write her regular *Peverel Papers* for the *Catholic Fireside* magazine. In the latter, we can see the style developing which was to make *Lark Rise* such a success more than ten years later.

Fact or Fiction?

Those familiar with her work will recognise her habit of fictionalising the truth—when she wrote about the life of 'Laura' in *Lark Rise*, it was of course about herself, Flora. She tells us of her family and the people around her, while changing their names and, to some extent, their history. This technique became an issue for Oxford University Press when they wished to take her work, since they did not normally publish works of fiction. But, recognising the merit of the book, they accepted it—and such was the demand from readers that they soon commissioned the sequels which became *Over to Candleford* and *Candleford Green*.

It is interesting to consider why Flora wove fact with fiction in the way she did. Sometimes it may have been to protect her own feelings, and sometimes to protect the feelings of others. It also allowed her the liberty of putting true events into more readable contexts—we know of several instances where a good yarn was reused in another piece of writing—and on her own admission she sometimes combined the characteristics of two or more people into one for the purposes of making a story.

But we should remember too that she wrote her main works more than forty years after the events she was describing—and who among us can remember precise details over that period of time?

So from the perspective of the local historian, her works have to be treated with care if used as sources of factual information. Her descriptions of life, particularly the life of ordinary rural people at the time of her youth, are considered to be some of the best available, and there is little doubt that the flavour and most of the detail which she gives us is entirely accurate. And yet if we try to relate her works to certain known historical facts, we can sometimes find ourselves on shaky ground.

'Heatherley' discovered

While investigating the history of my own part of the country, that area of the west Weald where the three counties of Hampshire, Surrey and Sussex all meet, I tried to take Flora's legacy and add it to our other pieces of local knowledge. The work of chief interest to me was *Heatherley*, which she wrote as a sequel to *Candleford Green*. It is truly the 'fourth volume' of the *Lark Rise* trilogy, taking up the story of 'Laura' the year after *Lark Rise to Candleford* finishes and describing her period in Grayshott. But for some reason she decided to leave it in typescript form, and started instead on what was to be her last work, *Still Glides the Stream*, which was not a continuation of 'Laura's' story. This she completed in August 1946, less than a year before she died, and it was published posthumously in 1948.

The texts of *Heatherley* and her other unpublished works were seen by Margaret Lane soon after Flora's death, and mentioned by her in a biographical essay published in the *Cornhill Magazine* in 1957. But it was not until 1970 that Anne Mallinson, who had a specialist country bookshop in Selborne, Hampshire, visited Flora's birthplace, read a copy of this essay and realised its true significance to the literary heritage of her own part of the country.

Here, along with Gilbert White, William Cobbett, George Sturt, WH Hudson and Edward Thomas, was another local 'rural writer' describing times gone by. And when the centenary of Flora's birth came round in 1976, not only were there celebrations in Juniper Hill—but Anne made sure there were celebrations also in Liphook, where a 'literary lunch' was held in the *Royal Anchor* attended by Margaret Lane among others.

Alerted by the celebrations of the centenary, the Bramshott & Liphook Preservation Society worked with Anne Mallinson to honour Flora's memory in the village more permanently.

In 1978 a plaque was placed on the wall outside the old Liphook post office where she had lived, and in 1981 a sculptured bust by Philip Jackson was unveiled outside the Portsmouth Road sorting office, and subsequently moved into the village Library in 1995.

Although the biographical essay was reprinted once more for the centenary, the full text of *Heatherley* still lay in archives which had by that time been deposited at the University of Texas. Margaret Lane was encouraged to retrieve a copy of the typescript and prepare it for publication. This she did, including also some of Flora's poems and extracts from her *Peverel Papers* nature notes, producing the book mentioned earlier, *A Country Calendar and other writings*, published by Oxford University Press in 1979.

Only then did the people of Grayshott discover that, along with Arthur Conan Doyle, George Bernard Shaw and the other eminent writers who had based themselves in and around the village at the turn of the century, there had been yet another literary talent living unknown and quietly among them. These great men of letters had used her post office, and she had sold them stamps and handled their telegrams, all the time listening to their conversation and wishing 'that one of those quick, clever remarks they tossed like coloured balls into the air could have come her way.' But it never did so—and not one of these men recognised that a kindred spirit stood serving them behind the counter.

Though she stayed in Grayshott for only two years or so, it was a significant chapter in Flora's life—her 'Sinister Street' years, when she felt she had first become an adult woman—and perhaps *Heatherley* tells us more about the character of the author than do her more famous writings. Could this be one reason why she chose not to publish the work herself?

You must judge for yourself as we follow in her trail....

County boundary stone in
Crossways Road, Grayshott.

left side: H = Hampshire, Headley
right side: SF = Surrey, Frensham

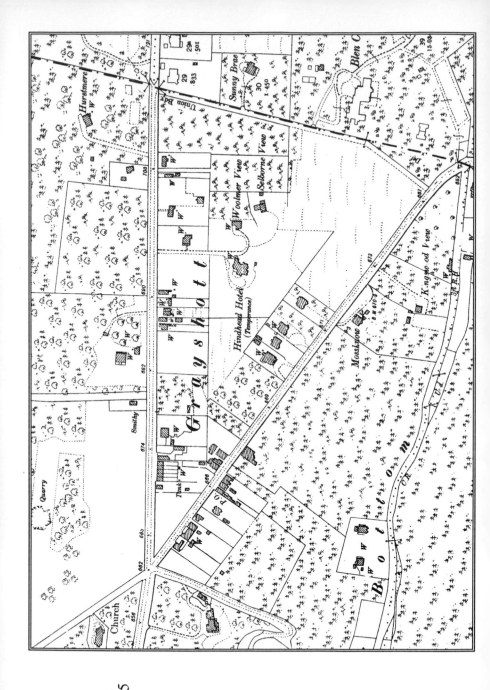

Centre of
Grayshott
about 1895

'Laura' goes Further

ઌ ઌ ઌ

CONTENTS

Crossways Road,
Grayshott about 1900.

Right foreground:
W. G. Chapman,
joiner & cabinet maker,
which was also the
Post Office where
Flora worked

To Grayshott

Grayshott came as a surprise to Flora. Sometimes she felt that she had strayed into a different world, more prosperous and leisured, but less kindly than that of her birth. She had grown up in a village where everybody knew everybody else, but here she was in a new settlement less than a generation old. What had previously been wild heathland was now becoming 'developed'. John Tyndall, an eminent physicist of the time, had declared the air to be 'as pure as that of the Alps' and, now that the railway in nearby Haslemere gave easy access to London, a number of other distinguished men and their families had followed his lead and moved to live in the nearby hills. The village of Grayshott existed largely to serve their needs.

The landscape, too, was completely different from that which she had been used to as a child. Instead of heavy, earthy scents and flat cornfields stretching away to a distant line of trees, here was the sharp tang of pine trees, the sweet smell of gorse and heather, and glorious views from the hill tops. She was struck by this when she first arrived, on a hot September afternoon in 1898. The Grayshott postmaster, whom she refers to as 'Mr Hertford,' had failed to meet her at Haslemere Station—she later discovered it was due to one of his regular domestic disputes—and, leaving her luggage to be collected later, she walked the three miles up to the village by way of High Pitfold.

As she came out of this tree-shaded sunken lane which led up to the open heath, she was astounded. There before her was spread a carpet of heather, stretching as far as the eye could see. She tells us that: 'Pale purple as the bloom on a ripe plum, veined with the gold of late-flowering gorse, set with small slender birches just turning yellow, with red-berried rowans and thickets of bracken, the heath lay steeped in sunshine.'

This was the scenery which had also captivated the co founder of The National Trust, Octavia Hill, just a few years before. She had been taken up the same track by one of the other co-founders, Sir Robert Hunter who lived locally, and literally gasped with delight when she saw the view. Sadly, although much of the land around Grayshott was later protected by their Trust, this particular view was not, and by 1949 it was reported that 'anyone who drove up High Pitfold today would see only masses of fir trees more or less concealing houses and gardens.'

Although Flora was standing in Surrey at the time, this first view of heathland became, ironically, her indelible image of Hampshire. Her destination lay half a mile away across the county boundary, and subsequent moves in her life were to acquaint her with other equally heather-clad parts of Hampshire.

Flora tells us that she walked into Grayshott on a 'hot September afternoon,' and we know from another source exactly what the weather was like that month. In the diary of Winifred Storr, aged 12, who lived nearby with her family at *Highcombe Edge* in Hindhead, we read that during the first twenty days of that September it was often 'almost too hot for words.' But on Wednesday 21st, the good weather broke, and towards the end of the month it became much colder with some torrential storms.

We are also told in *Heatherley* that 'Laura' was 'about twenty' when she arrived—in reality Flora was in her twenty-second year. She walked into the village from High Pitfold along Crossways Road and entered one of the detached tile-hung shops situated on its south side, from which Walter Gillman Chapman, her 'Mr Hertford,' traded as Joiner and Cabinet Maker. Here he also ran the village post office as 'a sideline to supplement his main income.' Flora was employed by him to be 'in charge of the office' and, with the help of a junior assistant, was to 'undertake all the postal and telegraph duties and make up the daily accounts' which had then to be signed by him.

The person she was replacing, a woman of forty whom she refers to as 'Miss Smithers,' looked as if she was on the verge of a nervous breakdown. She told her before leaving the next morning that the household Flora was joining 'was far from a happy one,' and that Mr and Mrs 'Hertford' had what she described as 'terrific bust-ups,' although to her there 'never seemed any sense or reason in their quarrels.'

'I expect it's just that she doesn't know how to manage him,' she said to Flora, 'it's generally the wife's fault in such cases.'

Postal Services to Grayshott

The first postal deliveries to Grayshott started in 1864, coming on horseback from Bramshott to Edward I'Anson's house, with the few residents of the village (population then less than 100) collecting their letters from him. The first shop in the village was nearby, being run by Henry Robinson and his wife Hannah from the late 1870s. They moved to higher ground in Crossways Road, then known as 'Upper Grayshott,' and built a shop there which became the first post office in 1887, designated a sub-office of Petersfield.

Edgar Leuchars, a London architect like I'Anson, had in 1880 built a 'summer house' for himself and his young wife here, and pressed for a telegraph office to be opened in the village. He achieved this—in 1890 a notice appeared in the local paper stating that: "Telegrams are now received for transmission at the Grayshott Post Office. By residents at Hindhead & vicinity this is much appreciated."

But Henry Robinson's tenure as sub-postmaster was not without problems, and in 1892 he was effectively sacked from the job. A note in the Post-Master General's minute book of 28th May that year reads:

"The Telegraph duties at the Grayshott Post Office of which Mr Robinson is the sub-postmaster, are performed in a most unsatisfactory manner.

"It appears that no proper attention is given to the Telegraph instrument and that irregular remarks to other offices on the circuit are constantly made by the assistants.

"These assistants are the sub-postmaster's son and daughter over whom he seems to have no control, the son being allowed to write insolently worded reports on his father's behalf in reply to enquiries from his superior officers.

"As there seems to be no chance of improvement whilst the office is in the hands of the present sub-postmaster, I submit that it be declared vacant as proposed."

The Robinsons' son Peter George was 16, and their daughter Ruth 15, at the time of the offence.

Walter Chapman was appointed sub-postmaster in July, and the office moved to his shop a few doors along Crossways Road. He was to retain the position for nine years until he, too, was forced to move on—but for very different reasons.

'The Hertfords'

Flora tells us of the first time she met 'Mr Hertford', shortly before the office closed on the evening she arrived. 'She had not heard him come into the office; he wore soft-soled shoes which made no sound, and she turned suddenly to find him standing behind her, laughing silently at her start of surprise.' She says he was 'a dark, slightly-built man of forty-five who might have been thought handsome but for the peculiar tint of his complexion, which was a deep, dull mauvish-leaden shade, and the strange wild light in his eyes. The silent laughter was a habit of his, and another disquieting habit was that of quoting texts of scripture or lines from the poets in a hissing whisper. "Vengeance is mine ..." or "To be or not to be ..." he would hiss under his breath, *à propos* of nothing that had gone before, when taking up the pen to sign the account, or even at the family meal table.'

'But in spite of these and many other peculiarities,' Flora says that in several ways she liked him. 'That evening he welcomed her cordially, and he was reasonable in his business relations and an expert at his trade.' She tells us that he 'took no part in local affairs and seldom came into contact with ordinary post office customers, many of whom were under the impression that Laura was postmistress and addressed her as such.'

'He was a master of debate,' she says, 'and to hear him and his brother, who lived near, discuss politics and theology was a revelation to one who had gained such little knowledge as she possessed from the printed word. His brother was a non-conformist in religion, a devoted chapel-goer; Mr Hertford attended neither church nor chapel and, as far as could be gathered from his ordinary conversation, was a sceptic; yet in these debates he would contend hotly for an established Church.' During the Boer War, 'Heatherley had its pro-Boer in the person of Mr Hertford's brother, who proclaimed his principles by growing a beard and wearing a wideawake hat, similar to those worn by the Boers in pictures.' Mr Hertford himself, 'rather surprisingly, had come out as an ardent supporter of the war.'

The Chapman brothers were born at Barley in Hertford-shire—hence perhaps Flora's choice of the pseudonym 'Mr

Hertford' for Walter. Ernest had first come to the district some twelve years previously, in about 1885, and started a building firm. He was a staunch Congregationalist, and is the 'Mr Hertford's brother' to whom Flora refers in *Heatherley*. Walter had settled in Grayshott 'on the advice of his brother who was in business and doing well there.' He is not shown in the census of 5th April 1891 for Grayshott, but local sources indicate that he was at the premises which Flora describes in Crossways Road by the following year, just across the road from his brother Ernest's builders yard.

In that same year, 1892, a third and younger brother, Oliver Chapman, also moved to the village and became Ernest's shop manager and general assistant. He is never mentioned by Flora, surprisingly perhaps, since he must have been a regular visitor to her 'Mr Hertford' and, by all accounts, was a bit of a 'character.' Moreover she had good cause to remember him when looking back over the years, for reasons which we shall come to later.

Walter himself was a bachelor when he moved to Grayshott, unlike his two brothers, but Flora tells us that soon afterwards he had met 'Miss Mosley,' and that when his housekeeper left, 'Miss Mosley' took her place. Six months later, she says, they were married. We know from parish records that 'Miss Mosley' was in fact Emily Revelle, who married Walter on 13th November 1892 in All Saints' Church, Headley, which was the parish church of Grayshott at the time. He was 36 years old, she was 28, and the witnesses were Oliver Chapman and his wife Sarah Jane. Her father's name is given as Henry Kirk Revelle, occupation Contractor, and there is a Chapman family legend which says that her side of the family were of Huguenot stock and involved in the glass industry. Some five years later, in July 1897, her much younger sister Florence then aged twenty-one married Frederick Deas, son of the Grayshott grocer. She was living in Liss at the time, but moved to become a near neighbour of Emily's by the time Flora arrived in the village, though there is no mention of this sister in *Heatherley*.

'Mrs Hertford,' Flora tells us, was 'unusual for her time and position in life. She was tall, thin and faded, with drooping shoulders, a very pale face, and smooth straight masses of dull yellow hair which she wore combed low over her ears. She was in a late stage of pregnancy and wore a long loose green frock with much embroidery about the shoulders. Her voice was melancholy and her movements were silent and slow.' Flora thought her face was 'the saddest she had ever seen.' She seemed to care nothing for the subjects which interested her husband, her passion being music, and 'in her rare hours of domestic peace she would sing or hum airs from the operas.' But only once during the time Flora knew her did she go out to a concert, and after that occasion 'her husband had one of his wildest outbursts of temper and she went to bed weeping.'

A twenty-seven-year old woman named Annie E Revell is recorded in the 1891 census working as a housemaid for Professor Alexander Williamson, one of the 'eminent men' of the area, at Upper Pitfold House. Her birthplace is stated simply as Suffolk. Could she be our Emily? Flora tells us that 'Miss Mosley' was a nursery governess to parents who had taken a furnished house in the area one summer. Perhaps Emily took on this role in the summer of 1891, or perhaps Flora's version is not strictly accurate—or perhaps they are two completely different people.

According to Flora, 'Mr Hertford' had come to Grayshott after spending many unsettled years in Australia, and his wife once confided to her about the life he had led before she met him. It was, Flora says, 'the kind of story beloved of minor Victorian novelists'. He had apparently been 'born the son of an inn-keeper, had had a grammar school education and been apprenticed to what in those days was considered a superior trade, that of cabinet-maker; but when in his late teens he had fallen in love with the daughter of a well-to-do farmer, her parents had forbidden the match as most unsuitable and derogatory.' The girl, whose name was Letitia, or Letty for short, was stopped from seeing or writing to him openly, but they managed to make a secret pact that he should emigrate to Australia 'where men of his trade were said to be making fortunes in large towns,' and then 'having saved a sufficient sum from his earnings, he should return to England and claim her hand.'

For three years while he was out there, he 'had only to stoop to pick up money' as Flora herself had heard him say, such were 'the demands of those who had made their fortunes in gold-

mining and were bent upon furnishing their newly-built houses.'
They were fond of 'large, ornate pieces of furniture, richly
carved,' and he had 'a noticeable talent for such work.' Then, at
the age of twenty-two, having earned enough and booked his
passage home, 'he received a cable from his parents: "Return at
once. Letty ill. Her father consents to marriage." It was during
the hurry and excitement of the few following days that he had
the heat-stroke which so badly affected his after life.' By the
time he landed in Southampton he had apparently recovered, but
an even greater shock awaited when his father met him with the
news that Letty was dead, and he returned 'not to a marriage,
but to a funeral ceremony.'

'Mrs Hertford' told Flora that he had 'probably made some
vow to himself then never to marry, but to remain true to the
memory of his lost love.' At any rate, she said, when he
proposed he had told her: "I'll marry you if you will have me,
but my heart is buried in poor Letty's grave." And Flora tells us
of seeing a photograph of a 'slim, sloping-shouldered girl with a
pork-pie hat perched on a chignon of fair hair which hung on the
wall of Mr Hertford's bedroom. For he had his own bedroom,'
though the arrangement 'did not appear to interfere with the
regular arrival of his children.'

The Chapman family today cannot verify Flora's story of
Walter's unrequited love for 'Letty', but they can confirm that
he visited Australia on several occasions. They are not sure
about 'heat-stroke' being the cause of his unstable mental
condition in later life—another family legend blames a glass
lemonade bottle which exploded in his face sending a sliver into
his brain. But he was certainly a well-respected craftsman.
Flora mentions that he 'carved and fitted the woodwork of a
private chapel in the house of a Catholic resident' in Grayshott,
almost certainly for Mr & Mrs Vertue at *The Court*, which is
now the *Cenacle* convent. He is also said to have carved the
altar for the new Grayshott parish church of St Luke's which
was consecrated in October 1900, and during one of his periods
in Australia he reputedly carved the doors of the Melbourne
parliament building.

When Flora first knew the 'Hertfords' they had, as she says,
a boy and a girl. The boy Walter George, to whom Flora refers
as 'Cecil,' was aged 3½ and the girl, Florence Louise (known in
the family as 'Lulu'), was nearly 2 years old. Another boy and

girl were born while she was there (although Flora herself mentions only the girl)—these were Thomas Gillman born on 1st March 1899, and Ethel on 6th June 1900. And finally, Ernest James was born on 16th June 1901, after Flora had left the village.

She tells us that 'in some ways she had never before been so near happiness as during her first few months at Heatherley. She had work she enjoyed, a new countryside to explore, plenty of books to read, and some interesting people to observe. The one disadvantage was her position as one of the Hertford household.' She had been offered accommodation with the Chapmans in the post office until she could find a room of her own, because 'humble lodgings' were difficult to find in the village. But she soon found that all too often she became an embarrassed third party in family disputes between Walter and his wife. Also she would sometimes 'wake in the night and hear soft, padding footsteps on the stair or in the passage outside her bedroom, and more than once or twice she awoke suddenly with the impression that someone had been standing beside her bed.'

Feeling very much alone in the world, Flora remained there all through her first winter in Grayshott, but things came to a head one night after she had gone to bed and 'heard a loud bang which she thought at first was some kind of explosion. Rushing out onto the landing she found Mrs Hertford in her nightdress, coaxing her husband back to bed. He held a small revolver in his hand, and Mrs Hertford afterwards told Laura that he had thought he heard whispering beneath the landing window and, thinking it was burglars, had fired his revolver to scare them away.'

Whether or not the shot scared anyone else, it certainly scared Flora, and she found herself lodgings elsewhere within a week.

However, she continued to work at the post office during the day, and occasionally heard 'the old sounds of strife' from within the living quarters while she was operating the telegraph machine. In fact during the whole of her time at Grayshott, she says, 'even in moments of personal happiness, she was aware, if dimly, of a sinister cloud in the background.'

'Alma Stedman'

The one person who helped to make those early days tolerable was 'Alma Stedman,' her junior assistant in the post office, whom Flora describes as 'a pretty, blue-eyed, sweet-natured girl of eighteen whose home was in the village.' She was, says Flora, 'good and sincere, untouched by the world and its problems and yet no fool, with inborn good taste and a sense of humour, and was one of those rare persons who are happy and contented and wish for no change in their lives.' She had a 'bright, sunshiny nature,' whereas Flora, 'as people told her, was too much inclined to look on the dark side of life.' When 'Alma' saw her brooding, she had 'pretty, innocent ways of trying to cheer her which, though often simple to silliness, would usually raise a smile.' Sorting the night mail, she would read out addresses on the letters pronouncing the place names grotesquely, or hide Flora's ring, or shut up the office cat in the registered letter locker.

Her real name was Annie Symonds, and her children are happy to confirm that Flora's description of their mother's 'sunshiny nature' in *Heatherley* is absolutely accurate. She had arrived in the village in November 1892 from her native Cheshire at the age of fourteen, when her father John Symonds came down with Mr Marshall Bulley, related to the founder of Bees Seeds, to be his gardener at Hindhead. The Bulleys lived with Miss James at *West Down*, and the Symonds family moved the following year into *Fir Cottage*, which is at the end of the path now belonging to the National Trust and known as *Miss James' Walk*. From here, it was about a half mile walk across the Portsmouth Road and down *Pollock's Path* to the centre of Grayshott. Annie attended Grayshott village school for a few months, and worked for a while as a pupil teacher there, then eventually took a job as junior assistant at the post office.

One of Flora's first duties was to teach her how to work the single-noodle telegraph machine which had been 'newly-installed.' Until she mastered this, Flora herself had to cover all twelve working hours in the office each weekday, from eight to eight, and two hours on Sunday morning. After that, it was agreed that they should finish work on alternate evenings at six o'clock. Life at the time, Flora says, 'ran to the tune of its musical tinkling' as the machine struck out Morse code 'which could be heard and interpreted, by those accustomed to it, at some distance from the instrument.'

What Flora liked best about Annie was 'that she was a reader and especially fond of poetry,' particularly works which 'had a touch of magic or faery about them.' Her favourite poet was Christina Rossetti, and she also introduced Flora to the works of Coventry Patmore. But, unlike Flora, Annie had not discovered these authors herself. As Flora puts it: 'Although her taste was inborn it had not gone uncultivated.'

Mrs Bulley, the wife of Mr Symonds' employer whom Flora refers to as 'Mrs Camden,' was a well-known personality in the village and ran a Sunday afternoon class of poetry-reading for 'a few selected girls,' of whom Annie was one. 'The only drawback,' says Flora, was that whatever Mrs Bulley liked, Annie liked 'so much that she was not inclined to venture further, certainly not to trust her own taste and judgement. She had the advantage of knowing on good authority what books and poems were worthy of her love, but she missed such thrills as Laura experienced when, having come casually upon some book or poem and loving it, she afterwards learned that it was an acknowledged masterpiece.'

Annie's taste in everything 'ran to the small and exquisite,' says Flora. 'The violet and the snowdrop were her favourite flowers and, as a view, she preferred some mossy nook with primroses blooming against tree boles to the wide, purple expanse of the heath in its glory.' About such things the two of them would 'contend a little,' as Flora puts it, and she tells us that because of this she wrote for Annie the poem called 'Heather,' which begins:

> *You talk of pale primroses,*
> *Of frail and fragrant posies,*
> *The cowslip and the cuckoo-flower*
> *that scent the spring-time lea,*
> *But give to me the heather,*
> *The honey-scented heather,*
> *The glowing gypsy heather—*
> *That is the flower for me!*

This became one of the poems which Flora included in her collection *Bog Myrtle and Peat*, published some twenty years later.

'Eminent People'

Grayshott was ahead of neighbouring settlements, and in particular ahead of Hindhead, in having the telegraph facility installed. As a result, many of the 'eminent people' who lived in the area came to use Flora's office, and she tells us of her 'restricted post-office counter view' of them all. 'Some were brilliant conversationalists,' she says, 'and when two or more friends or neighbours met there, it amused her to listen to their talk. She would sometimes wish that one of those quick, clever remarks they tossed like coloured glass balls into the air could have come her way, for in her youthful vanity she persuaded herself that she could have caught and returned it more neatly than someone to whom it was addressed.'

On her first Sunday morning walk, she saw 'a tall man on a crutch with a forked red beard and quick, searching eyes' surrounded by a group of younger men 'who appeared to be drinking in his every syllable.' This was George Bernard Shaw, who was living in *Pitfold House* at the time, having rented it in June of that year from the Beveridges, both to spend his honeymoon and to convalesce from a badly infected foot. Apparently, as soon as the foot improved he threw away his crutches and took to his bicycle again. However, being rather accident-prone where bicycles were concerned, he fell off and sprained his ankle, which was why, when Flora saw him, he was on his crutch again!

Later that year he moved closer to the village centre, renting *Blen Cathra* for a period of eight months until he moved away from the area in August 1899. During this time he worked on *The Perfect Wagnerite* and *Caesar & Cleopatra*, and also became thoroughly involved in a number of local activities. Flora herself tells of attending some of the addresses which he and others gave at the nearby Hindhead Congregational Hall, on such topics as: *Why I am a Socialist, Being a Vegetarian,* and

Disarmament. Chairing one well-attended meeting on 28th January 1899 on the subject of *Disarmament* was Arthur Conan Doyle, who had moved into his newly-built *Undershaw* across the road from the Hall just over a year before. Shaw later declared in typical fashion that he had 'cured Conan Doyle of sentimental pacificism and left him a raging Jingo' by his speech that day.

In the year that Flora arrived in Grayshott, Annie's elder brother Jack was working for Doyle at *Undershaw*. While maintaining the Diesel engine which powered the house, he had been overcome by fumes and had collapsed with his leg pressed against the hot exhaust pipe. He was not found until the next morning, by which time the leg was so badly burned that it had to be amputated.

Annie told her children that her father had walked from Hindhead to the hospital at Guildford several times to see him, including the day of his 21st birthday. She also recalled that Doyle had paid their family money in compensation.

Flora remembers Doyle as follows: 'Scarcely a day passed without his bursting like a breeze into the post office, almost filling it with his fine presence and the deep tones of his jovial voice. As he went through the village he had a kindly greeting for all, rich and poor, known and unknown alike. He was probably the most popular man in the neighbourhood.' He had moved to the area, like so many others, to take advantage of the supposed health-giving properties of the air. In his case, it was his wife's health that was the cause for concern, since she had contracted tuberculosis. While living here he wrote most of his *Brigadier Gerard* stories and, in order to earn some money, resuscitated Sherlock Holmes from his premature demise at the Reichenbach Falls.

While in the area, Doyle became interested in spiritualism and the exploration of occult phenomena, but on a more practical level he was also involved in local sporting activities, being described by a contemporary as 'a man with a hand that grips you heartily and, in its sincerity of welcome, hurts.'

He served as a physician in the second Boer War, and his pamphlet justifying Britain's action earned him his knighthood in

1902. He was also one of the first motorists in the area, and in that same year bought a 10HP Wolseley, driving it himself from Birmingham to Hindhead. His first wife, Mary, died in 1906 aged 49 and is buried in St Luke's churchyard along with their son Kingsley who died of wounds in the First World War.

Conan Doyle re-married in 1907 and moved to Crowborough in Sussex.

Another author using the post office at the time was Grant Allen. He, like Doyle's wife, suffered from TB and had come to Hindhead for the air. He published *The Woman Who Did* and *The British Barbarians*, his so-called 'Hilltop Novels,' while living here in 1895, and these caused a storm of protest in the press and elsewhere. Flora says: 'Everybody who knew the author by sight, or even the outside of the house he lived in, felt a burning desire to read his book, and copies were bought and handed round until practically everyone of mature age in the village had read and passed judgement on it.' But she continues: 'Some who had secretly enjoyed reading his novel seemed quite disappointed when the pother it had caused died down and the author still walked at large, apparently unperturbed by the storm he had raised.'

Allen had intended to write a series of 'Hilltop Novels,' but on 25th October 1899, as young Winifred Storr recorded in her diary: 'Our poor dear friend and neighbour Grant Allen died this morning at about 12.15 a.m.' Other sources say that Conan Doyle, who had moved to Hindhead largely on Allen's advice, was by his bedside at the end.

A fourth author mentioned by Flora was 'the young poet whose work was then held in high esteem in literary circles,' and who 'raced about the parish at all hours on his bicycle with his halo of long, fair hair uncovered and his almost feminine slightness and grace set off by a white silk shirt, big artist's bow tie and velvet knickerbockers.' This was Richard Le Gallienne, then in his early thirties, who had also 'found' Hindhead on the recommendation of Grant Allen, and was living in *Kingswood Firs*, just above Waggoners Wells, at the time Flora saw him. He had published one of his more famous works, *The Quest of the Golden Girl*, a year previously but, as Flora says, because of the other 'locally revered figures' such as Tennyson for whom 'the whole neighbourhood felt an almost proprietary interest, this new young poet, who actually lived at Heatherley, was little regarded locally.' He left the village in the autumn of 1900, and later went to live in New York.

Of these four authors, only 'Mr Bernard Shaw' is actually named by Flora in *Heatherley*—not when she is first introducing us to him, but only later in the book. She mentions some other writers by their real names, Tennyson for one and George Macdonald for another, both of whom had lived nearby. She also talks of going to hear Ian Maclauren, the Scottish novelist, read from his 'then very popular book' *Beside the Bonny Briar Bush* at Hindhead Congregational Hall, and she recalls going all the way to Box Hill one summer Sunday just to see the outside of the house where George Meredith lived. However, none of these people ever used her post office and, with the exception of Shaw, she preserves the anonymity of those who did.

ೀ ೀ ೀ

The Enclosure of Grayshott

Until the enclosure of Headley Common was completed in 1859 (incidentally the same year that the railway arrived in Haslemere), the area now known as Grayshott was part of an expanse of uninterrupted and largely lawless heathland stretching from Haslemere through to Farnham and beyond.

In 1861, the architect Edward I'Anson bought some land here, built a house (at the location which is now the *Cenacle* convent), and moved in with his family from Clapham. He was considered brave by some and rather foolhardy by others, as he had been given warnings that the bands of ruffians operating in these parts, would never allow a stranger to settle among them. But he stayed, apparently unmolested, and soon became a leading figure in the future development of the village.

A few years later, in 1867, Alfred Tennyson rented Grayshott Farm (where Grayshott Hall now stands) for about a year while his new house *Aldworth* was being built near Haslemere. He too wrote of being warned about the local inhabitants, but his short stay was also uneventful, and he was charmed by the peace and quiet he found in the surroundings.

The Diary of Winifred Storr (1885-1971)

Winifred was the second daughter of Rayner Storr (1835-1917) by his second marriage, and named after his first wife who had died in 1877.

Her father had retired from the family firm of London auctioneers at the age of 36, and by 1897 was living with his family in *Highcombe Edge*, a large, newly-built house overlooking the Devil's Punch Bowl at Hindhead. (A local press-cutting of 15th October 1896 notes that Ernest Chapman was the contractor and Oliver Chapman the superintendent of joinery during the construction). The Grant Allens, the Conan Doyles and the Bernard Shaws were regular visitors to her family.

Rayner Storr was active in local affairs, becoming vice-president of Grayshott cricket club and Undershaw football club, and President of the Grayshott & District Refreshment Association which ran the *Fox & Pelican* when it opened in 1899. He was also one of the enthusiasts who in 1888 had started the *Haslemere Natural History Society*, which Flora eventually joined when she returned to the area in 1916.

Although brought up as a Methodist, he became an adherent of Positivism, a movement which respected equally the objectivity of science and the idealism of religion. His second wife, Alice Severn, was already a Positivist, and his children, including Winifred, eventually followed this persuasion too.

The diaries kept by Winifred during 1898 and 1899, when she was twelve and thirteen years old at *Highcombe Edge*, give us details not only of the weather each day during those two years, but also of the comings and goings in the Storr household. Kingsley and Mary Doyle—Arthur Conan Doyle's children—in particular visited her for parties and played cricket with her. She also mentions walking and cycling down to Grayshott several times to visit the post office there for stamps, postal orders and Christmas cards—but no mention is made of the assistant post mistress!

Winifred eventually married Gerald Brooke (of Brooke Bond) and they had three children. It is to one of them, Mrs Anna Powell, that we owe the safe-keeping of her mother's diary.

'The Wind on the Heath'

Once Flora had taught Annie the workings of the telegraph machine, she was able to spend more time pursuing what she called 'another interest which lay nearer to her heart's core'— namely her love of nature. She tells us that 'her greatest pleasure in life was in her few free daylight hours to roam on the heather-clad hills or to linger in one of the valley woods where trickling watercourses fed the lush greenery of ferns and bracken and mosses and the very light which filtered down through the low, matted undergrowth was tinged with green.'

These were solitary walks, unlike those she took with her friends when there would be 'a brisk swinging progress from point to point to the accompaniment of much talk and laughter.' When alone she could 'stand and gaze at some favourite viewpoint, watch the heath birds and insects and quick-darting lizards, gather the heath flowers into little stiff honey-scented bouquets, run the warm, clean heath sands through her fingers and bare her head to the soft, misty rain.'

She tells us that 'Sunday morning, after the office had closed was the best time, and in winter the only time for solitary walks. With good luck in the matter of work, she would have her hat and coat already on when the telegraph instrument ticked out its daily message from Greenwich: *T-i-m-e — T-i-m-e — T-i-m-e*, then after a few seconds' pause, *T-E-N*! A moment later she would have locked the door behind her and be halfway down the village street on her way to the hills or woods. Looking neither to right nor left lest she should see some acquaintance who would volunteer to come with her, she would rush like a bandersnatch, as someone once said who had seen her from a distance, and take the first turning out of the village which led to the heath.'

Here 'when she felt the heather brush the hem of her skirt and breathed the honey-scented moorland air, she was filled with a sense of freedom and detachment from ordinary life such as she was never to know elsewhere.' But young single ladies in those days were not supposed to go walking on their own, and village tongues naturally wagged. Occasionally she was followed to see

34

who she met, but the pursuer would most likely be disappointed to find that her interests were entirely virtuous, and to most people probably quite boring, as she strode along sandy tracks, brushed through thickets, or picked her way carefully through marshes, always observing, and always adding to her store of knowledge about the natural world around her.

She does not identify by name any of the places she visited, but it is clear that the lakes which she says 'were one of the sights of the neighbourhood, always visited by strangers and have since been bought by the National Trust,' were in fact Waggoners Wells. Although a favourite place for picnickers even in those days, Flora says she seldom found anyone other than herself there on Sunday mornings. She mentions the Wishing Well, 'at that time a deep sandy basin fed by a spring of crystal clear water which gushed from the bank above,' and tells us of the local belief that anyone drinking the water would have their wish granted, provided they dropped in a pin. There were, she says, dozens of pins to be seen rusting on the sandy bottom of the well in those days, quite a number of them dropped in by herself.

On returning to Grayshott twenty years later, when she lived in Liphook, she says that the well was 'much altered, a house had been built a few yards from the path and a garden wall stood on the bank.' The spring water no longer gushed forth in a crystal stream but fell in a thin trickle from a lead pipe, the sandy basin had been filled in, and she found that no-one she met in the neighbourhood had even heard of a Wishing Well. 'After its centuries of existence,' she says, 'it had disappeared, and the memory of it had faded from men's minds.'

Flora might be glad to know that the Wishing Well has since been restored, though not in its original form, and that coins collected in it now find their way to the National Trust.

There were occasions when she came upon other human beings during her wanderings—the man she called 'Bob Pikesley' was one. He was a commoner who grazed his cows on the heaths during the day and took them back home to his smallholding in the valley at night. He taught her the secret of keeping dry under pine trees when it rained, showed her her first adder, and told her many other practical points of country lore. She describes him as 'short of stature, and his slightly hunched shoulders drooping forward caused him to appear shorter than he actually was; the skin round his shrewd grey eyes was drawn into wrinkles by his outdoor life, and he wore the earth-coloured garments of poverty on the land.'

Flora says she 'at first took him for a labourer, herding the cows of another, but although he lived the life of a labourer, in all essentials Bob was his own master. He was a small freeholder with commoner's rights and lived in his own cottage with a widowed sister.' She described their home as being 'so tucked away between two hills that it was possible to pass within a hundred yards of it without suspecting its existence. It was a narrow thatched cottage with outbuildings in a valley so narrow that their three fields were ribbonlike in length and breadth. As Bob said, you could throw a stone from one hill to another right over the chimney and never know that a house was there.'

Who 'Bob Pikesley' and his sister 'Jeanette' really were we may never know—indeed they may well be composite characters built from a number of people Flora had met at different times in her life. But she does give us a clue, which again comes from the time she was living in Liphook, when she 'discovered by chance that the woman who came in to clean for her was a native of Heatherley.' On asking about 'Bob' and his sister, she was told that 'Jeanette' had nursed her old mother through her last illness and looked after the house and dairy, then both she and 'Bob' had died 'in that influenza epidemic, as they called it, just after the war. Both down with it at the same time and nobody to look after them.'

Local burial records show only one pair of people dying of the post-war 'flu within days of each other, this being Albert Alderton and his wife Emily, who both died of 'flue & pneumonia' in February 1919 according to the Headley register. He was 51 and she 47 years old, and they lived in Whitmore Vale, a narrow, tree-lined valley which fits almost exactly Flora's description of where the 'Pikesley' farm was. To add to this evidence, the Rector's notes also state that Emily had been looking after her mother during a long illness just before she died. Were they the 'Pikesleys'?

We are not sure which of the several small farmsteads dotted along the length of the valley was theirs, but it was presumably on the Hampshire rather than on the Surrey side of the county boundary, or the rector of Headley would not have included them as parishioners. However, if the Aldertons really were Flora's 'Bob and Jeanette,' then they were not brother and sister as she described, but husband and wife.

'Mr Foreshaw'

Flora was, as she put it, 'fairly well versed in the ways of the earth, but untrained in the ways of the world,' and did not understand the suspicions which some of the villagers held towards her expeditions and encounters. Even Annie was a little taken aback by Flora's strange choice of companions, especially when it came to the retired big-game hunter whom she calls 'Mr Charles Foreshaw.' He was 'a distinguished-looking old gentleman with snow-white hair and a small, neatly-trimmed white beard' who Flora often noticed at the post office counter. Annie told her that a year or two before he had had a bungalow built for himself at the end of a little lane off the main road, since when he had lived there alone—but that was all she knew of him. Flora was intrigued, 'loving a mystery, and being exceptionally fond of aged people' as she says she was.

'Disregarding rules and regulations, she would take the letters from his awkward, arthritic old hands and stick on the stamps for him.' Then one evening in August, after office closing time, a telegram arrived for him, and Flora, after some hesitation, delivered it to him herself. This was the start of a firm friendship, and after that, Flora tells us, she went to see him at least once a week for nearly a year. 'On many Sunday afternoons,' she says, 'she sat opposite him at the table at which she had first seen him sitting over his maps, and ate guava jelly, dried ginger, or some other dainty he had brought out from his store-cupboard, with cream in her tea, while he drank black coffee and nibbled a dry biscuit.'

From the first, she liked him 'for his originality, his raciness, his immense store of experience and his biting wit, and as she came to know him better and realised what a trial it must be for him to live such a quiet, inactive life after his years of stirring adventure, old and alone and often in pain, her liking deepened to affection.' He showed her his many trophies and specimens, and almost every article in his collection had a story attached to it, often of a 'narrow escape from wild animals met suddenly in unexpected places, from snake bite, or from hostile native tribes.' And, of course, they discussed their favourite authors, including Kipling, Dickens and Thackeray, and books on travel and biography, and particularly on Africa.

Flora remarks that 'looking back in after years, she was surprised that she learned so little about his life. He would talk freely about his thirty years of big-game hunting in Africa, but of his life before and after that period he said not a word. Where he had been born and spent his childhood, who were his parents, and whether or not he had relatives still living at the time she knew him, she was not told.'

But then one morning, 'the news ran around the village that the old gentleman up at the bungalow had died in his sleep. The ex-serviceman who cleaned and cooked for him had found him looking as peaceful as a child asleep, and the doctor had said that it was no more than he had expected, as the rheumatic complaint affected the heart.'

According to her, the doctor and a lawyer from town were the only mourners at his funeral, and their two wreaths were the only ones placed on his coffin. 'To those wired, waxen florist's flowers, when they lay on the grave,' she tells us, 'another friend added a bunch of red roses, chosen because she knew he had loved deep, rich colour in flowers, as he had loved everything strong, warm and positive in life.'

The bungalow and its contents were sold by auction, and she says that on the day of the sale she watched people passing by the post office window carrying the items she recognised. She made a timid attempt to buy back his copy of *Vanity Fair*, but the lady who had bought it was not willing to sell. It was some small consolation to her that his collection of butterflies and some of his native weapons and pottery were bought by the curator of a museum. Those at least, she thought, would be kept together and not 'knocked about.'

The local museum at Haslemere does indeed hold a notable butterfly collection, but has no record of any of these being bought at such an auction.

Flora was both saddened and sobered by his death. It was, she tells us, the first time in her life that she felt such a personal loss. Previously 'people she had known had died and she had felt sorry, but none of them had been near to her; she had never before faced the great dark, silent abyss which lies between the dead and the living.'

There are few positive clues as to who 'Mr Foreshaw' might have been. However, Flora does indicate that he was buried locally, and only one man in the surrounding parishes' burial records seems to come close to fitting his description. This is John Volckman, who died on 10th August 1900, aged 63, and was buried in the churchyard at All Saints, Headley. The note against his name in the register states: *'of 3 Chichester Street, St. George's Square, London SW - Stranger at Grayshott - friend is A.L. Pike.'*

An obituary in the *Surrey Advertiser* adds the information that the Rev J.M. Jeakes of Grayshott officiated and the chief mourners included Miss Volckman (sister), Mr Arthur L Pike (nephew), and Mr H.A. Swepstone (solicitor to the deceased).

His will, dated May 1899, bequeathed all his property to his sister Helen, widow of John Michael Shum—and one of the few things that Flora had noted about 'Mr Foreshaw's' private life was that he had a sister. She tells us, using her pseudonyms, that an inscription on the fly-leaf of one of his books had read: *'Charles Foreshaw, from his loving sister Clara. Christmas 1880.'*

Unfortunately no other information is yet to hand confirming whether or not John Volckman was 'Mr Foreshaw,' and attempts to trace living relatives have so far proved unsuccessful. His death certificate, signed by Dr Arnold Lyndon, adds that he was 'of independent means,' and that the cause of his death was 'Diabetes 3 years, diabetic coma 20 hours.'

But if it was he, then we may perhaps visualise Flora walking the three miles from Grayshott to Headley on Sunday 19th August 1900, her first free day following his death, to lay red roses on his grave—a grave lying unmarked in the shadow of the mediaeval church tower; a peaceful resting place for him indeed.

'The Jeromes'

It was probably at about this time that Flora became acquainted with her 'Bohemian' friends, a couple whom she refers to as 'Mr & Mrs Jerome.' She had for some time, she says, 'noticed with interest, and always on a Saturday, a rather peculiar looking couple at the post office counter. The husband, 'Wilmot' was a large, tall man, past the prime of life, decidedly aristocratic looking, and with a voice and accent closely resembling that of elderly Victorian gentlemen in BBC broadcast plays.' His wife, 'Alicia' was a complete contrast. 'She was much younger, small, and what was then called "dressy," and her English, though that of an educated woman, had a slight Cockney accent. She had been pretty in her youth and her features were still good, but, as such small, fair women so often do, she had worn badly.'

Flora tells us that 'Mrs Jerome' was schoolmistress in a neighbouring Hampshire village, and he was a writer of short stories, who preferred to post his manuscripts from Grayshott rather than his own village post office where the inquisitive 'Mrs Garbitt' would gossip about it. They became friendly when Flora helped 'Mrs Jerome' to fix the quill in her hat during one of their Saturday visits, and soon afterwards she was being invited over to their house every Sunday after the office closed, to stay the rest of the day. Here she was introduced to the world of journalists, some of whom used to 'run down from town' on a Sunday to see 'Mr Jerome.' The men would sit at the table for hours talking shop, and Flora says she would not have missed a word for worlds, 'and when "the Street" or the office of such-and-such a periodical were mentioned casually, she was puffed up with pride at the thought that at last she was moving in literary circles.'

The 'Jeromes' had been childhood sweethearts who had drifted apart, and Flora tells us the romantic story of how they found each other again late in life, after 'Alicia' had already taken up the post of schoolmistress. In those days a woman teacher was expected to resign her appointment upon marriage, and so they wed secretly 'in the nearest large town.' But their situation was soon discovered, and the clergyman who was one of the school managers interviewed 'Alicia' and had to be told the truth. He, personally, was against the compulsory retirement of married school teachers, Flora says, and promised to use his influence with the county authorities to make an exception in her case. Apparently, by the time Flora left the area no decision on her retirement had yet been reached.

In trying to identify the 'Jeromes,' we first considered in which neighbouring Hampshire village 'Alicia' was most likely to have been schoolmistress; the choices being Bramshott, Liphook and Headley. The nearest of these is Bramshott, some 2½ miles away as the crow flies, though the walk is not a straightforward one, as those attempting Flora's Trail at the end of this book will testify. The others are both about 3 miles away. Flora says that 'Mr Jerome' insisted on walking her home from their house in the evenings, but it is hard to believe that, even in those days, a man 'past his prime,' as Flora said, would walk such distances just to escort a young lady home.

No local reference can be found to the case of a married schoolmistress being taken up by the authorities at that time, and we are left with no sure clue as to who the 'Jeromes' might have been, or indeed if they were real people at all. Flora, it seems, decided not to include their story in the final version of *Heatherley*. Her chapter about them appears to have been typed only in draft form. Could this indicate an uncertainty about them on her part?

The 'missing chapter' is printed in full later in this book—see 'From the Archives.'

The post office in neighbouring Headley was run by the Gamblen family at this time, who used to put up the village schoolteachers as lodgers. Ten years before, as recorded in the 1891 census, their boarder was Miss Mary West, aged 24, born in Oxford, who later married Mr Edwards, a previous headmaster of the village school.

It seems unlikely that Mr and Mrs Edwards could be Flora's 'Jeromes,' but it is possible that Mrs Gamblen may have been in her mind when she wrote of 'Mrs Garbitt.'

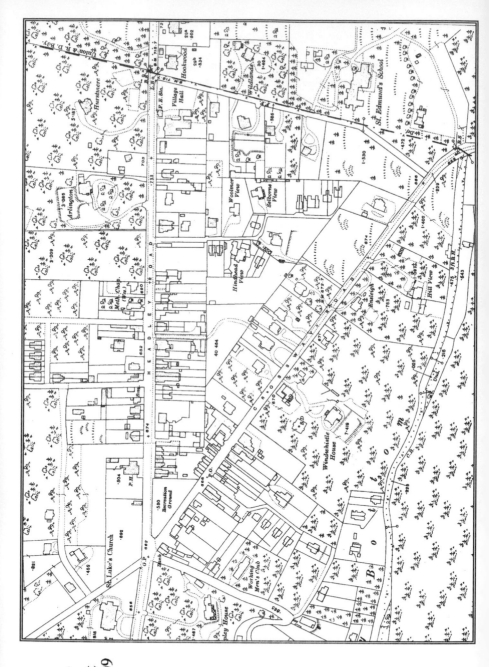

Centre of
Grayshott
about 1909

The Businesses of 'Heatherley'

ᘒᘒᘒ

Flora mentions her 'immense ninepenny dinners' being a feature of the 'new model inn' at Grayshott. This was the *Fox and Pelican*, opened by the Bishop of Winchester's wife in August 1899, a great occasion which brought many notables to the village. It was called a 'Refreshment House' rather than an inn, because the intention was to 'supply alcoholic drinks of a good and reliable quality, whilst at the same time allowing the villager or passer-by to buy a good and cheap cup of coffee, a plate of meat, and bread and cheese, or any other refreshments he might require.' The manager was to receive commission upon the sale of non-alcoholic drinks only.

A number of the 'eminent men' of the neighbourhood had been involved in promoting this project, chief among them being Sir Frederick Pollock, a distinguished lawyer, who chose the name of the inn from 'the conjunction of a site in Bishop Fox's diocese (Winchester) with a chairman who was a member of his own foundation (Corpus Christi College, Oxford) whose symbol is the Pelican.' Walter Crane of the Royal Academy painted the signboard, and George Bernard Shaw, teetotaller that he was, supported the scheme and donated a small library of books to the establishment.

Flora was a great borrower and reader of books. She does not mention Shaw's bequest, but she did use the library facilities at 'Madam Lillywhite's' in Victoria Terrace, conveniently just across the road from the post office. She tells us that she almost 'read her head off,' as her mother would have said, getting through everything she borrowed so quickly that she was often ashamed to return a book so soon. She was also a writer who 'felt throughout her life a sense of some duty neglected which almost amounted to a feeling of guilt whenever her pen was idle.'

However, as a result of her coming to Grayshott and having seen, and to some extent known, those she thought of as 'real writers,' she had felt 'ashamed of her own poor attempts' and for a while gave up trying to write. Even her journal, begun on the day she first left home, was abandoned—presumably the 'penny exercise book' which, she says in *Over to Candleford*, was presented to her by her brother Edwin. She destroyed that 'along with her other scraps of writing, saying to herself as they smouldered to tinder that it was the end of a foolish idea.' We are left to guess how long it was before she began writing again.

Flora says of 'Madam Lillywhite' that she was 'a small, elderly, daintily dressed lady who must have had a passion for her stock of real lace, for she was always adorned with collars, cuffs, jabots and other furbelows of that delicate material. Over her picturesquely dressed grey hair she wore draped a lace shawl in the style of a Spanish mantilla.'

Her real name was Fannie Warr, and apparently she did like to be known as 'Madame Warr.' Flora tells us that the other tradesmen in the village thought her 'decidedly odd' for it, but that Madame herself did not seem to care.

The Rector of Headley recorded in 1898 that he had received a note from Mrs Warr passed to him by a neighbouring clergyman, in which she asked him to buy some of her needlework in order to help with her finances. In it she says, "A little longer and then what I have been struggling for all these years will be accomplished (the bringing up of my large family by needlework, etc). I often look back and wonder I have got thus far without income, health, husband or anything that other people have to fall back on; and do feel I have 'stuck' to them through great difficulties." He does not say whether or not he bought any! Fannie Warr died in 1915 aged 66, so she would have been about fifty at the time Flora referred to her as 'elderly.'

Flora does not tell us very much about the other shopkeepers of the village, although there were more than two dozen shops and other businesses there at the time. We hear the story of 'Marion,' a large, serious, moon-faced girl from the sweet shop, who suddenly found she had to speak at the next Christian Endeavour meeting and asked Flora and Annie for help in composing her speech. Flora casually suggested 'The Sweets of Life' as a subject, and says that 'Marion' adopted the idea with enthusiasm, but when, a few days before the talk, she had still not written more than a minute's worth of text, it was Annie, not

Flora, who finally took pity on her and went round to help her finish it.

But of other village businesses we hear very little. Nothing, for example, of Alfie Wells, the blacksmith in Headley Road who was, according to one account, 'a great consumer of pints of beer, and plied his trade in a splendid shower of sparks and a wealth of language, often profane.' Nor of Mr Hoy the fishmonger, with his slogan "Fresh Fish every Morning;" nor Mr Coxhead with his ironmongery business (one of the few premises to have remained in the same trade to the present day); nor Mrs Hart and her sweetshop (unless Marion belonged to her); nor Mr Frost, stationer, barber, and collector of "night soil;" nor any of the occupants of the shops next to the post office in Crossways Road such as Mr Prince the baker, Mr Munday the greengrocer, Mr Upex with his off-licence, or Mr Deas the grocer.

Nor does she mention the carriers, on whom Grayshott depended before the days of public transport. There was John Sandall, who arrived in 1893 and started the first carrier business in the district—but it was said of him that he operated rather spasmodically, and had difficulty passing a pub without stopping. And there was Stephen Boxall, the broomsquire and hawker of whortleberries, who had a very large black horse and whose cart acted as hearse for funerals at Headley, there being no churchyard at Grayshott until past the turn of the century. The coffin rested in the cart, and any mourners unable to walk the three miles sat on the cart rails. Doubtless 'Mr Foreshaw' would have travelled to his final resting place by this means.

Several broomsquire families lived in the area—they were, in a way, the original residents of the site on which the village grew—and Flora mentions their 'little low houses with ricks built of the few handfuls of hay from their fields and the other much larger and taller piles, built rickwise, of new heather brooms with shining white, newly-peeled handles, ready to be taken to market' to be sold at three shillings a dozen.

She also tells us of an incident, which we know happened in May 1900, concerning a particular broomsquire whose house she used to by-pass on her walks on account of his ferocious dog. 'There had for some weeks been an epidemic of dog-poisoning,' she tells us. 'There were many such barking dogs in the neighbourhood, for at that time and in that district ignorant people thought a watchdog made a better guard if kept constantly on a chain, and one by one they were found in the morning dead before their kennels, poisoned.'

James Belton, the broomsquire in question, and his brother Henry decided to hide at night and keep watch over their collie. At about midnight, a figure approached the kennel with a piece of meat, which later turned out to have been laced with strychnine. The Belton brothers rushed from cover and seized him, finding that the man they had caught was, according to Flora, 'a much respected doctor who had a large house on the border of the heath' and who was running a nursing home for patients with nervous disorders. She tells us that his house was 'a few hundred yards distant' from the scene of the crime, which happened in Stoney Bottom. We know from the subsequent trial and press reports that the man was Dr Coleclough. He was fined £10 with £5 costs, and within a few months had, not surprisingly, left the district.

'*Richard & Mavis*'

A visitor to the village who influenced Flora's life perhaps more than any other during her time at Grayshott was the man she calls 'Richard Brownlow.' He entered her post office 'one winter afternoon when the oil lamp which swung over the counter had been lighted at half-past three and all who had no urgent business to compel them to face the east wind were enjoying their tea and muffins by the fireside.' She describes him as 'a large young man, both tall and thickset, with a snub nose and remarkably clear bright grey eyes' and a face 'whipped into rosiness by the wind and rain. His small fair moustache and the shaggy grey surface of the overcoat were beaded with raindrops, and he carried a stout walking stick of some natural wood.'

She guessed at first that he was a farmer or a game-keeper, but says she was 'wide of the mark' in this. He had spent almost the whole of his life in London, she tells us, although he was not a Londoner by birth. For the last few years he had been employed by one of the big cable companies. He had come to stay with some 'connections by marriage' who had recently settled in the village, and wanted to send a telegram to tell his mother of his safe arrival.

Flora tells us he was 'evidently a cheerful and communicative young man.' He was also about her own age, and she must have given some sign of having been attracted to him, for when she said to Annie later that she 'didn't think she had seen that young man before,' Annie answered, "You'll see him again!"

And she did. During his first short visit to Grayshott, she tells us he called at the post office 'several times daily,' and after that he was 'frequently down for weekends and longer holidays.' The friendship which was soon established between them, she says, grew rapidly. They shared much in common including a love of literature. 'If one of the two began to quote poetry, the other capped the quotation, or held out a finger to link and called out the name of the poet to signify that their thoughts had been identical.'

'Richard' had an only sister 'Mavis,' who sometimes came with him to Grayshott. Flora says they were devoted to each other and their tastes were alike. 'Both were fond of ideas, especially ideas for reforming the world, and they were aware of and deplored social ills (though they had no plans for their redress); both loved the country and both were well read.'

'Mavis,' she says, was quite unlike 'Richard' in appearance. While 'Richard' was large, she was 'a slender graceful little creature with dark red hair, eyes the colour of autumn beech leaves and a velvety cream complexion. She was so small and dainty of build and so quick and bird-like in her movements that beside her Laura, herself neither large nor inactive, felt clumsy.' In mental qualities, she 'did not reason things out to a logical conclusion as Richard did, but reached her conclusions by flashes of insight or by wheeling and dipping in a kind of swallow flight which, light and casual as it might appear, was certain.'

Flora was delighted by her new friends, she tells us, not only for what they were in themselves, but also because they were *modern*. 'They had the latest ideas, knew and sometimes used the latest catchwords, and had read and could discuss new books by new authors whose names, to Laura, were but vaguely familiar.' She describes how 'on dark nights, after the post office had closed, they would take long walks, swinging along the highway, Mavis on Richard's arm on one side, Laura on the other, chanting in unison the quatrains of Omar Khayyám, or a chorus from Swinburne, or talking sense or nonsense.'

They visited the cross on top of Gibbet Hill at Hindhead, where Flora says she 'dropped to her knees on the turf and, pressing her ear to the cold stone of the shaft, recited in trance-like tones an imaginary conversation between two malefactors who she asked them to suppose had once suffered there, an effort which was applauded as worthy of Poe.' Flora says that it was she and 'Mavis' who would exclaim the tragic lines of verse into the night, while 'Richard,' tall as a cliff and firm as a rock between them, 'preserved the mental as well as the physical balance by keeping mainly to passages from Milton or Shakespeare.'

On Sunday afternoons and light summer evenings, Flora 'showed her friends some of her moorland and woodland haunts.' Some, but not all; there were a few spots she held inviolate as her secret sanctuaries, including the 'oblong of lawn-like turf, threaded by a little stream, and shut in on every side by trees and thick undergrowth,' which she called 'the heart of the wood.' This was where she had hurried away on at least one occasion, to hide 'with hot, angry tears in her eyes' when a slighting remark she had received reminded her that she had 'neither the birth, education, nor any personal quality to justify the holding of an opinion differing from those held by the majority.'

She found that 'Richard' and 'Mavis' loved the country and never tired of exploring its beauties, though, unlike her, they studied it consciously, never resting until they could name each bird or flower, while she drew a more instinctive interest in its enveloping atmosphere. One day, far out on the moors, she introduced them to a curious parasitic plant, showing them 'a patch of heather which, from some short distance, looked stunted and blighted and had a reddish tinge. When closely examined, every individual plant was seen to be netted and dragged down to earth by thin, red, threadlike runners.'

The plant is called *dodder*, and Flora declared that, 'if she were a novelist, she would write a book with that title. It would be the story of a man or woman—she thought a woman—of fine, sensitive nature, bound by some tie—probably marriage—to one of a nature which was strong, coarse and encroaching, and would tell how in time the heather person shrank and withered, while the dodder one fattened and prospered.'

Dodder—*Cuscuta epithymum*

A most curious plant, with leafless, tendril-like stems. Individually scarcely noticeable, these stems can swamp a clump of Heather or Dwarf Gorse with a tangled mass of lurid pink and yellow threads *(see p. 70)*.

Dodder lacks green pigment because it is a parasite, drawing nourishment through sucker-like modified roots which are firmly attached to the stem of another plant. It is rooted in the ground only as a seedling.

from a Field Guide to Wild Flowers

It is tempting to think that Flora might have been referring to her own marriage to John Thompson when she wrote this passage, some forty-five years after the event she describes. We may also sense that, given different circumstances, Flora and 'Richard Brownlow' could have become more than just good friends, but it was not to be. Flora gives us the background to 'the shadow' on the Brownlow home life which eventually resulted in 'Richard' moving out of her life.

She says that five years earlier, 'Richard and Mavis's' father had died suddenly in bed by the side of their mother, who had been so shocked that her nervous system had been shattered and she had been left more or less an invalid. 'Richard, at that time not quite twenty and Mavis eighteen, had been left alone to face hitherto undreamed-of responsibilities.' After a while, their mother's recently widowed elder sister, 'Aunt Maggie,' was able to come and relieve them of the housework, allowing 'Mavis' time to learn shorthand and typing with a view to a post in the City. She also suggested that the pair of them needed a 'change of air' and suggested 'Richard' went for a long weekend to 'a nephew of her late husband' who had shortly before gone to live in 'Heatherley.' This was how 'Richard' had come to meet Flora.

We are told that he and 'Mavis' were 'anxious that Laura should get work in London,' and persuaded her to pay a guinea and begin studying for a Civil Service examination. But Flora tells us she 'knew from the first she could not hope to win even the lowest place in a competitive examination, no matter how hard she studied. Her education had left too many blank spaces and, apart from that, she had not a competitive mind.' She had to leave most of the arithmetic problems unsolved; and although her geography was a little better because she had read a good deal about foreign countries, and in essay writing she was able to reach an average mark, or sometimes a little above the average, her handwriting alone was pronounced 'satisfactory.' The comments of her coach, she says, were not very enlightening, but there was a human touch on one occasion when she took as her essay subject *The Portrait of a Lady* by Henry James. Below the official red-ink assessment she found written, 'A curious choice. Don't care for James's work myself, but almost thou persuadest me!'

'In the Cage'

Another Henry James story, *In the Cage* written in 1898, imagines a young girl confined daily to a little cage in a branch post office at the back of a Mayfair grocery store, handling the cryptic telegrams of the outer world, counting the words and reckoning the fees. She takes in the meaning of the messages, and they tell her of certain scandalous goings-on in society.

Almost certainly Flora would have read this new work of James' while she was in Grayshott.

Flora's new friends invited her up to London one weekend, and met her when she arrived at Waterloo station on the Saturday evening. 'Each seized an arm and dragged her through the, to her, immense and confusing crowd on the platform,' and out to sit on the open top of a horse-drawn bus for the journey to the family's flat, which was situated in 'a pleasant suburban road.' She tells us it was the first time she had seen London or any large town by night, and 'she found herself gazing down with deep interest on the flaring shop-fronts and the crowds surging before them,' and smelling the thick, moist air which appeared to her to taste of 'a blend of orange-peel, horse manure and wet clothes, with a dash of coal gas.'

'To be actually in London for a night and a day in the company of her brilliant friends was exciting to Laura, and to be cared for and made much of was comforting to one who lived far from her own home and was dependent on herself alone for her well-being.' But although the aunt was a 'perfect angel,' Flora found the presence of their mother 'disquieting.' Her manner to her was, we are told, 'polite, though by no means cordial,' and when Flora finally arrived back in Grayshott the next evening and 'breathed in the pure, invigorating air with conscious enjoyment,' she tells us that she 'rejoiced in her sense of release from the flaring lights and eddying crowd,' and, we suspect, also the release from 'Mrs Brownlow.'

The next day she wrote to the Civil Service college saying that she had decided to 'discontinue her course at the end of that session.' After that, she says, 'there was a slight, indefinable change in the relationship' between herself and her 'Brownlow' friends. 'Every month or two, Richard and Mavis would come to Heatherley for a weekend, or Richard would come alone on a Sunday and return the same night,' but 'the shade of a shade' had crept between them. It hurt Flora to know she had disappointed them, and all was not quite as it had been before.

Then, one winter evening when Flora was locking up the post office, already muffled up ready for the dash home, she was surprised to see 'Richard' standing outside on the pavement. He signalled to her to come out, and when she did his first words to her were, "I want to talk to you." Her room, having a bed in it, was quite out of the question as a meeting place, she tells us, and so they walked in the dark through the fog and slush towards the main road. Here 'Richard' felt for her arm and, 'as they moved slowly along the main road,' told her that 'Mavis' had been examined by a doctor who had told their Aunt Maggie that 'although there was no positive symptom of the disease, he felt he ought to warn her that her niece's condition showed a marked tendency to tuberculosis.'

'Richard' already felt a responsibility towards his widowed mother, and after this latest news he realised his obligations were doubled. 'She's going to have the best possible treatment,' he told Flora, 'even if I have to borrow money from a moneylender. One day you'll read in a newspaper, "Young man in money-lender's clutches!" and you'll find you know that young man.'

Then he startled Flora by saying to her, 'I can never marry, you know that, don't you?'

Flora says she stiffened inwardly at this, thinking, 'Good Heavens, surely he doesn't think I want him to marry me!' We can only imagine where the truth really lay. She says she told him as lightly as she could, 'But you don't want to marry anyone, do you? And perhaps by the time you do you'll have made a fortune.' She left him there at the crossroads, where High Pitfold meets the Portsmouth Road, for him to walk down to Haslemere and catch the ten-thirty train. 'Still enveloped in fog,' she tells us, they 'stood beneath the signpost, her hand in his hand. All had been said that could be said and their few moments' silence was filled by the sound of water dripping from the boughs, and the humming of telegraph wires. They parted, and she stood for a few seconds listening to his retreating footsteps. Then the sound ceased for a moment; he turned and came back at a running pace, but all he had to say when he reached her was a last "Good-bye, Laura".'

Flora records that 'Richard and Mavis' both came back to see her once more 'during the summer,' but it was a farewell visit as she was then 'leaving Heatherley to take up a post fifty miles farther from London.' She tells us that the three friends 'never met again', and gradually the letters which passed between them 'grew fewer and farther apart.' She never found out what happened to 'Mavis,' but feared that 'that bright, high-spirited young life was not to be a long one.'

However, 'of Richard she did hear once more. Many years after he and Mavis had passed out of her life, Laura's youngest son, then an engineering apprentice, passed to her over the supper table one of his technical journals for her to look at the illustration of a new liner which had just been launched, and there, on turning the page, she read an account of a presentation to Richard on his retirement from the service of the cable company.'

'A portrait of the once familiar face looked up at her from the page. It was that of a prosperous, kindly-looking middle-aged man, clean-shaven and a little inclined to plumpness; but the eyes which gazed straight out of the portrait at the beholder were Richard's eyes, keen, steadfast, and slyly humorous, and the smile on the lips was Richard's old smile. He had been on the company's business for some years in China, and other sojourns of his in the far east were mentioned.' She also tells us of the 'cottage on the east coast where it was hoped he would spend many years of well-earned retirement,' but there was no mention of a wife, and Flora says she felt 'some regret that their ways in life had been so far asunder.'

In trying to track down the real 'Richard Brownlow,' we looked through back-copies of *Zodiac*, the internal magazine of *Cable & Wireless*, the most likely cable company to have employed 'Richard,' and here we found one report of a retirement which broadly fitted Flora's description.

William Burton Elwes OBE retired as Staff Controller on 30th March 1937 at the age of fifty-nine. He had joined the company in 1894, and served them in Singapore, Madras and Hong Kong before returning to a home posting in 1922. He was moving to 'a Georgian cottage overlooking a lovely valley' in Pett, East Sussex. His picture *(see inset, p.70)* also fits Flora's description of 'Richard.' Unfortunately, however, his service record placed him in Madras at the time Flora was in Grayshott.

Nevertheless, he looked too good a match in other ways for us to ignore entirely, and by searching through his Will we traced descendants of his sister, whose name was Lilian Bella. She had survived to marry Col. John Josselyn and bear children, and we were able to contact a granddaughter of hers, Audrey.

We asked her to read *Heatherley*, and she was immediately struck by Flora's description of 'Richard' first entering her post office—particularly the clear eyes, fair skin, and cheeks whipped into rosiness; also his love of countryside and an interest in knowing the right names for everything, and his concern about social injustice, but no plans for doing anything about it. "That's Uncle Bill!" she said. She also told us that he had come home for long periods of leave, and therefore the Madras posting did not preclude him from being 'Richard Brownlow.' Also that his sister was devoted to him, and that they did go around together as Flora said.

But there were other parts of the story which did not fit. For one thing, their father had not died suddenly—he had in fact been an Archdeacon in Madras, and died in 1924 at the age of 80. Also, Lilian was tall and elegant with blue eyes, not as Flora described 'Mavis.' She had never suffered from tuberculosis, and would not have considered doing anything so menial as working for a living. The family at that time, on the admission of today's generation, were 'a bit snobbish.'

'Uncle Bill' had been known as a 'bit of a flirt,' says Audrey, and was in demand with the ladies—but apparently always had to get the approval of his sister before starting anything serious! And this might be the key to our conundrum. Flora, it seems, is unlikely to have been regarded as sufficiently 'top drawer' for the Elwes family at the time, and if Bill's flirting with her began to look as if it was getting beyond a casual affair, Lilian may well have decided to put a stop to it. If so, then the excuse of 'Mavis' having an illness as the reason for 'Richard' pulling out could have been fabricated, either by Flora or by 'Richard,' to save face.

And why choose the name 'Brownlow' for him? It was a familiar surname around Grayshott at the time—there was, for example, a local magistrate of that name—but there are also two other intriguing possibilities: firstly, the word Brownlow can very nearly, with a bit of doodling, be made out of the letters of Burton Elwes; and secondly, there is today, not much more than a hundred yards from the spot where Flora said good-bye to 'Richard' under the signpost, a house called 'Brownlow'—it was built after her time in Grayshott, but may well have been there during her stay at Liphook and her subsequent pilgrimages to 'Heatherley.' Or is it just a coincidence?

Living Alone

When Flora made the quick decision to quit her room at the Chapmans, she moved in with a retired business couple and their grown-up daughter, a family to whom she gives the name of 'Binks.' They were 'in one of the villas just beyond the village street.' We have not been able to identify the 'Binks' family or their villa, but her stay with them was only a short one. Though kind-hearted, says Flora, 'Mrs Binks' had not much delicacy of feeling, 'several times pointing out to her what a great advantage it was to be permitted to share such a home as theirs, and for such a small sum weekly.'

It turned out that the real reason they had taken her in was as a companion for their daughter, 'Clara,' and Flora tells us that 'although Clara was all very well in her way, her way was not Laura's way and she had no wish to be forced into it.' She found she could never go to her bedroom to write a letter or read a book without a cheerful Cockney voice calling out some such invitation as: "Come on down, you poor lonely little thing and let's cheer you up a bit!." So when Flora heard of another room becoming available in the village, she made the excuse of wanting to live closer to the post office, and moved in with the 'Parkhurst' family.

Flora says she 'never forgot the feeling of exaltation she experienced when, her day's work done, she for the first time approached her new dwelling, saw the flickering of the firelight on an upper window, and knew the room in which the fire had been lighted was *her* room, in which she could shut herself without fear of intrusion.' She tells us it was 'a wild March night' when she first moved in, and after her evening meal she arranged her few possessions and sat up long after her usual bedtime enjoying her first taste of freedom for months.

Winifred Storr's diary for March 1899 says the windiest day of the month was Wednesday 29th, and there had also been a fair amount of snow on the ground a few days earlier. Just the right sort of weather to curl up quietly in front of a fire with a good book.

The house 'had been built by a speculating builder with the idea of attracting a superior type of purchaser or tenant; but as it had a very small garden and was closely neighboured by a group of poor cottages, he had for some time been unable either to sell or let it.' Finally it had been let to two working-class families, the 'Parkhursts' being one, occupying rooms on either side of the house. Flora rented a front room upstairs—this, she said, 'was a fair-sized room with two windows, one of them with a view of the heath and, in the distance, the long wavy line of blue hills she had seen on the day she reached Heatherley.' Here, 'for more than two years,' Flora stayed until the day she left the village.

The couple who rented the other part of the house had three small children, and 'Mrs Parkhurst' had three small girls among her seven children still living at home. These 'all ran in and out, or played in the hall or on the stairs in wet weather' so that 'neither housewife felt inclined to provide a stair-covering, and the bare boards, though frequently scrubbed, gave the place a poverty-stricken appearance.' This did not worry Flora, who

55

had come from a background of poverty, but concerned some of the kind ladies of the parish who felt it their duty to keep an eye on her, and who commiserated with her for being obliged to live in such a poor lodging.

These same ladies did not care much for 'Mrs Parkhurst' who 'had no time to attend Mothers' Meetings, even had she wished to do so, and indeed was not even a churchgoer.' She was too independent and forthright in her manner to please their taste, we are told, and 'calling as they did at odd hours and seeing her blowsed from housework, they put her down as a slattern.' Like Flora herself, she did not seem to 'fit in anywhere' with the regular pattern of village life. The family, Flora tells us, 'belonged to an obscure dissenting sect which had no meeting place nearer than that in a market town seven miles distant' and whose tenets were 'harsh and narrow.' Theatre-going, dancing, and novel-reading were counted as sins. Despite this she seemed to get on rather well with 'Mrs Parkhurst,' who appreciated the 'helping hand' which Flora was able to give her.

Her husband, we are told, was a 'tired-looking and trustworthy man, though not a skilled one,' who counted as one of his chief blessings that he had not been unemployed for a day since they married. Once a month, early on Sunday morning, he would come downstairs, dressed in his best and newly shaved, and set out on his long walk with a packet of bread and cheese in his pocket to eat between services. There he represented the entire family, since 'Mrs Parkhurst' and her younger children were unable to attend, her elder boys had no wish to attend, and the others 'had their own good ways of spending the Sabbath.' Twice a year 'Mr Lupton,' the minister of the denomination, cycled over to pay 'Mrs Parkhurst' a pastoral visit but, 'with commendable delicacy, always let her know beforehand when to expect him, and, in consequence, found Mrs Parkhurst dressed her best, the parlour swept and garnished and a suitable tea prepared.'

She was, as Flora describes her, a tall, massively-built woman of about forty-five, with dark hair and eyes, and well-defined features. 'Occasionally, when some passing excitement brought a faint flush to her sallow cheeks and caused her dark eyes to kindle, she might still have been thought a handsome woman, but constant childbearing and the strain of bringing up a large family on insufficient means had lined her face, sharpened her voice, and destroyed the contours of her figure.' Her ideas on dress, as in many things, differed greatly from Flora's. She did not presume to criticise openly what Flora wore or what she did, but would register disapproval by remarking somewhat sourly on things, and signify approval by a warmer welcome than usual, or by some small act of kindness.

She had been born and lived as a child 'in a hamlet near Selborne,' and was proud of her birthplace with its hangers and primroses, but when Flora asked her if she had heard of Gilbert White, 'Mrs Parkhurst' could only say that she thought she had heard the name mentioned at some time, but was not sure. She did, however, remember her hop-picking days there, describing them as the happiest of her life, and bemoaning the fact that whereas then 'the farmers were glad to let men off after the harvest was carried as it saved them paying out wages when there was nothing much doing for a week or so,' now there was no chance of going hopping, as a man who works for wages 'can't take a fortnight or three weeks off or somebody else would soon be stepping into his shoes on his job.'

Flora thought of the 'Parkhursts' as elderly people, since their eldest son was the same age as herself. They had a daughter away in service who was soon to be married, and they 'often spoke of themselves as getting on in years and how, as the younger children grew up, they hoped for an easier time for themselves.' But at the age of forty-seven, while Flora was still living with them, 'Mrs Parkhurst' found herself pregnant again. Her term ended with a long and difficult confinement, and young 'Elsie,' we are told, was born just a few days before Flora was due to leave the village.

In an earlier draft of *Heatherley*, Flora called her landlady 'Mrs Chivers' rather than 'Mrs Parkhurst' (see *From the Archives*), and it is tempting to assume that this was perhaps nearer to her real name than the one finally adopted. Certainly there was in Headley at the time a family called Chiverton whose members fit the ages and family size of the 'Parkhursts' reasonably well. The head of that household, Thomas, was a farm labourer, his wife Henrietta came from Greatham near Selborne, and parish records show ten children being born to them between 1875 and 1899, five sons and five daughters, the eldest son being just a year older than Flora, and the eldest girl aged 17 at the time Flora left.

But this family lived on the other side of the parish, some three miles from Grayshott, and we have no evidence to suggest they ever moved from there. Seemingly another example of a coincidence.

The precise nature of the 'obscure dissenting sect' to which the 'Parkhursts' belonged is also elusive. There are two market towns about 'seven miles distant' from Grayshott where they may have had their meeting place, these being Godalming and Farnham, and at twelve miles distant Petersfield is another possibility—certainly the Methodist minister, Mr Charles Phillips, used to come from there to Grayshott by train and foot before a Wesleyan church was opened in the village in 1902. He was a Primitive Methodist, and their tenets were indeed strict at that time.

Perhaps the release of the 1901 census will cast some light on the 'Parkhurst' (or 'Chivers') family, but until then their identity may remain a mystery.

Leaving 'Heatherley'

How long Flora would have stayed in Grayshott given her own choice in the matter we shall never know. Pressure had been mounting locally for telegraph facilities at Hindhead, and eventually they were installed, as reported in the Post Office Circular magazine of 4th September 1900. The office was just across the road from Conan Doyle's house *Undershaw*, and on the following day, Flora tells us, 'the number of telegrams sent and received at Heatherley went down 80 per cent.' (Hindhead handled sixty telegrams per day in its first week, according to a report in the local press). 'Laura's services were no longer needed; there was not sufficient work to keep her employed, and the postmaster's official remuneration in the new scheme of things barely allowed for Alma's smaller salary.'

Flora goes on to say that 'as soon as arrangements could be made she left Heatherley,' but we are not entirely sure when this was. It seems that it may have taken a few months to achieve, as she mentions the reaction of Annie Symonds and the people of

'Heatherley' to the Queen's death in January 1901—but she also writes of leaving the village 'on a sunny, misty August morning,' just after 'Elsie Parkhurst' was born, and she was certainly not around at the end of July 1901, when a dramatic village event occurred which we shall describe shortly; in fact she says that this happened 'a few months after' she had left.

Also at the time of this event, there was an assistant (Edith Henrietta Smith) working with Annie in the post office who had been there for 'about nine months'—she was possibly Flora's more junior replacement.

So did Flora in fact leave Grayshott in 1900, as soon as the Hindhead telegraph opened, and then invent the reaction of Annie and the others to the Queen's death when writing *Heatherley*?

The 1901 census, when available, will tell us where she was on the night of 31st March 1901. Until then, all we can say is that she seems to have left Grayshott some time between August 1900 and the Summer of 1901, 'transferring herself to another post office in a distant part of the county,' as she puts it, and thinking that she would never see 'Heatherley' again.

We can probably assume that the 'distant part of the county' to which Flora travelled, and which she had already told us was 'fifty miles farther from London' than Grayshott, was in fact Bournemouth. Her future husband, John Thompson, had been working there since 1891, when he crossed over from his native Isle of Wight at the age of sixteen to begin training as a sorting clerk and telegraphist. This was, coincidentally, the same year that Flora herself had started work, aged fourteen, at the post office in 'Candleford Green.'

Some researchers think that Flora may have already met John Thompson while she was at Grayshott, but there seems little evidence to support this, and she certainly does not mention it in her own book. There, in seven stark words, she simply tells us: 'A few months later she was married.'

She was in fact married more than eighteen months later, on 7th January 1903 at St Mary's, Twickenham—time enough for their friendship to have begun when she arrived in Bournemouth. But why marry in Twickenham? John Thompson's younger brother George, one of their witnesses, worked at the Central Telegraph Office in London at the time, and possibly Flora had taken a post there or somewhere else in the London area between meeting and marrying John—but this is conjecture. What we know is that John and Flora took up residence in Winton, a suburb of Bournemouth, early in 1903, and that their first child Winifred Grace was born there on 24th October of the same year.

A Village Murder

But though Flora had left Grayshott, our story must remain here for a while yet. She tells us of reading in a newspaper 'a few months later' that Walter Chapman had 'made a maniacal attack' upon his wife one morning as she bathed her newest baby, and had killed her. The event, which happened just before 10am on Monday 29th July 1901, was indeed well reported, the local paper adding that "the news, at first regarded as incredible and impossible, unfortunately proved to be only too true, and great excitement broke out in the village."

At the inquest, which took place in Grayshott two days later, Annie Symonds gave evidence that she had heard 'several screams, and being frightened as to the cause she ran to the front door and called for help.' In a draft for *Heatherley* which was not included in the book (see *From the Archives*), Flora tells of hearing that Annie had 'walked firmly into the room where the murderer still hung over his victim, took the baby from out of its bath and carried it to safety.' Walter's brother, Ernest, was just getting off his bicycle at his office across the road, and arrived in time to take Emily in his arms as she died. Walter, he said, had by that time retreated upstairs.

Dr Arnold Lyndon, who lived nearby in Crossways Road, testified to finding twenty-one puncture wounds in the body, and the four-inch long shank of a carpenter's carving tool so firmly embedded in her back that he had to use pincers to remove it. Under cross-examination at the trial he said that the brutal nature of the murder suggested insanity. He had been anxious about the mental state of Walter Chapman since November 1898, when Walter had made unfounded accusations about his wife's immorality and had referred to himself as being shadowed. It is interesting to note that Dr Lyndon's anxiety over Walter had occurred just a few weeks after Flora had started to lodge in their house.

The trial of Walter Chapman at the Winchester Assizes in November 1901 lasted less than two hours. He was declared guilty but insane, ordered to be detained during His Majesty's pleasure and taken to Broadmoor Prison, where he died in 1922. His five children were all cared for in the village—a Mrs Bramley of 3 The Villas, Grayshott was recorded as guardian of Ethel and Ernest when they started school in 1904/5—and on 15th March 1906, when the eldest child was eleven and the youngest four years old, all five were re-baptised in a single ceremony at St Luke's Church.

The office of Grayshott sub-postmaster was declared 'vacant,' but was not advertised in the Post Office Circular magazine. It seems that Walter's younger brother, Oliver, took the job over officially on 26th August 1901, and Annie continued to work there, eventually marrying Oliver's son, Harold, on 12th January 1910. Flora mentions that during her time there Annie had been 'spending much of her off-duty time with the young man she afterwards married.' If so, then her attachment to Harold was not just the result of his father becoming her employer, but it must have made the match more certain. She and Harold subsequently moved to the neighbouring Surrey village of Beacon Hill, just a mile away as the crow flies, and ran the post office there for many years.

When Flora visited Grayshott again after the First World War, she noted that Annie had 'married about the same time' as herself and was 'living away from Heatherley.' She must have known where, and for someone who 'made nothing of a ten-mile walk,' it would not have been difficult for her to have gone the extra mile to visit Annie there, but as far as surviving relatives know she never did. Perhaps it was because, as she says in her book, no close friendship had developed—they had remained as they had begun, upon friendly terms. And as Flora admitted of herself elsewhere, she tended anyway to be more attached to places than to people.

'Heatherley' = Headley?

At the time Flora lived in Grayshott the village was still part of the parish of Headley, so it is tempting to believe that her title *Heatherley* was simply a corruption of the parish name, and this may be so. It is also interesting to note, in the 1891 census, that there was already a house named 'Heatherlie' in Grayshott village, so someone else had much the same idea before Flora.

No. of Schedule	ROAD, STREET, &c., and No. or NAME of HOUSE	HOUSES			NAME and Surname of each Person
150	*Heatherlie (Headley Rd)*	*1*			*Charles S. Orridge Caroline Do*

The name Headley is thought to be derived from 'a clearing in the heath or heather,' so Heatherley is actually closer to the original meaning than is the current name of the parish. Among previous spellings recorded for Headley are *Hethleghe* (1269), *Hethelie* (16th century), and *Heathley* (18th century).

Walter Chapman's children in March 1902 – (L to R): Thomas 3; Ernest 9 months; Ethel 1¾; Walter jnr 7; 'Lulu' 5½; at Bryanston House, Grayshott

Written on the back of the photograph, which was sent to Walter in Broadmoor

Mr Walter G. Chapman.

For dear Daddie with Walter's love Mch 1912

Annie Symonds,
Flora's 'Alma Stedman',
aged about 17

Single-needle telegraph instrument
similar to that operated by Flora
and Annie in Grayshott

Flora, believed to be
in her early twenties

What Flora did __not__ say about 'Heatherley'

There was a great deal happening in the village, and indeed in the world at large, during the time Flora was in Grayshott, and she mentions much of it in *Heatherley*. The Boer War had started, bicycles and 'Brownie' cameras were coming into fashion, Socialism was advancing, and plans for bringing utilities such as gas, water and electricity into villages were causing arguments among ratepayers.

It was the question of water supply which finally caused Grayshott to split from its 'mother' parish of Headley in 1902, a year after Flora left. The more progressive population of Grayshott wanted it, while the more traditional rural population of Headley did not. It would be interesting to know which side of the argument Flora would have supported, given her rural background. The village finally got its water in December 1903.

Meanwhile Grayshott's first permanent church, St Luke's, was rising not a hundred yards from Flora's post office, the foundation stone being laid in 1898 by Miss Catherine I'Anson, one of the notable benefactors of the village. It was consecrated in October 1900 and, although today's imposing spire was not added until some ten years later, Flora would certainly have noticed this large stone building being constructed throughout the time she was there.

In the view of Mr J.H. Smith, writing in 1978, 'Grayshott was a late example of a village growing under the influence of a benevolent autocracy represented, though not exclusively, by the I'Ansons, the Whitakers, and the Lyndons.' They gave the village its parish church, village school, village hall, fire brigade and even its public house. George Bernard Shaw referred in 1899 to the work these people had done as 'rescuing the village from the barbarism of twenty years ago.'

Flora must have known them all, but she mentions their influence in only the most general terms. Her story is a personal one—about 'Laura,' the young country girl, confronting the end of her adolescence among unfamiliar people in unfamiliar surroundings.

Fox & Pelican in Headley Road,
Grayshott about 1900—the original pub
sign (right) was designed and painted by
Walter Crane RA

St Luke's Church, Grayshott
– built 1898-1900, while Flora was in the village
– without a spire until 1910

Grant Allen

Arthur Conan Doyle

*Some of the authors who used
Flora's post office in Grayshott*

Rayner Storr (photographed at Grayshott by GBS)

George Bernard Shaw

Richard Le Gallienne

The Gibbet Cross on Hindhead Common — 'One night when they had climbed to the sumit of a hill where a tall granite cross marked the spot where had once stood a gibbet, Laura dropped to her knees on the turf and, pressing her ear to the cold stone of the shaft, recited in trance-like tones an imaginary conversation between two malefactors … an effort which was applauded as worthy of Poe'

Wishing Well at Waggoners Wells today.

According to Flora, it used to be 'a deep sandy basin fed by a spring of crystal clear water which gushed from the bank above'

Opposite—Waggoners Wells, of which Flora says: —
'In autumn the foliage of the trees, red, yellow and russet, was seen in duplicate, above and upon the still, glassy surface'

THE PEACE CRUSADE.

SUCCESSFUL MEETING ON THE HINDHEAD.

SPEECHES BY WELL-KNOWN GENTLEMEN.

HINDHEAD & GRAYSHOTT.

WHAT SOCIALISM REALLY MEANS.

LECTURE BY MR. BERNARD SHAW.

Headlines to two of Sillick's articles covering meetings in Hindhead and Grayshott addressed by Bernard Shaw and Conan Doyle, early in 1899

William Austen Sillick, reporter at Grayshott for the *Herald*, pictured in the 1920s.

Flora describes him as having 'a sturdy figure, bright inquisitive eyes and head bent a little forward as though perpetually in search of news' and says 'there had been a time when he would even have risked losing an item of news' for the sake of a talk with her.

Dodder
on heather
and gorse

THE ZODIAC
CABLE AND WIRELESS LIMITED STAFF JOURNAL
April, 1937.
No. 345   Volume XXIX

William Burton Elwes OBE,
in retirement — was he
'Richard Brownlow'?

RETIREMENT OF
MR. W. B. ELWES, O.B.E.
(See Frontispiece).

MR. W. B. ELWES, Staff Manager, retired on
Pension on the 30th March, 1937.
Mr. Elwes, who was born in 1878, went to

It is within our knowledge that retirement has long
been in his thoughts and that many a summer day has
been spent in the car exploring the by-ways of Kent,
Sussex and Hampshire, seeking a nook deep in the
countryside, yet not too remote. Overlooking a lovely
valley in East Sussex in one of the most beautiful parts
of that delectable county, with a distant view of the sea,
he discovered a Georgian cottage—the cottage of his
dreams. Five-and-twenty years ago he wrote in these

London Road, Liphook, about 1914 — the post office is the single-storey building with arched windows; the postmaster's house adjoins it to the left; the *Green Dragon* is in the right foreground.

The Square, Liphook in the early 1920s. Note the bus waiting outside *The Royal Anchor* 'under the spreading chestnut tree' to leave for Alton. In her 'Peverel Paper' of July 1924, Flora writes of a bus journey she made 'through Gilbert White country' to a place where 'the hop gardens came into view' near her journey's end.

SUBSCRIPTIONS

FOR THE YEAR ENDING 31ST MAY, 1917.

Slater, Mrs. (paid in 1914-15)			
Sligo, The Marquess of	...	0 10 0	
Snook, Mr. H. V.	... ...	0 2 0	
Storr, Mr. Rayner (the late)	...	0 2 6	
Swanton, Mr. E. W.	... ...	0 2 6	
Swanton, Mrs.	... ...	0 2 6	
Talbot, Mr. G.	... ...	0 2 0	
Taylor, Miss	... ...	0 2 6	
Thompson, Miss F.	... ...	0 2 0	
Thorley, Mr. E. F.	... ...	0 2 0	

Flora subscribed to the Haslemere Natural History Society in 1917 & 18 and again from 1922 to 1927 —every full year that she was in Liphook except for the three in which she was occupied nursing Peter.

Part of Peter Redmond Thompson's birth certificate; born 19th October 1918 during one of the worst weeks for 'flu deaths locally

'Postie,' Louise Woods, as sketched by her granddaughter (right) and as she really appeared in her GPO uniform (below).

JAN 18 1915   JAN 18 1915   *Original*

ATTESTATION PAPER.   No.
Folio.

CANADIAN OVER-SEAS EXPEDITIONARY FORCE.

QUESTIONS TO BE PUT BEFORE ATTESTATION.
(ANSWERS).

1. What is your name? ..... *John Mumford.*
2. In what Town, Township or Parish, and in what Country were you born? ..... *South End Essex England*
3. What is the name of your next-of-kin? ..... *James Mumford.*
4. What is the address of your next-of-kin? ..... *126 North Road, South End Essex England*
5. What is the date of your birth? ..... *15 Dec 1892*
6. What is your Trade or Calling? ..... *Labourer*
7. Are you married? ..... *No*
8. Are you willing to be vaccinated or re-vaccinated? ..... *Yes*
9. Do you now belong to the Active Militia? ..... *Yes 27° Reg"*
10. Have you ever served in any Military Force? .. *No*
    If so, state particulars of former Service.
11. Do you understand the nature and terms of your engagement? ..... *yes*
12. Are you willing to be attested to serve in the CANADIAN OVER-SEAS EXPEDITIONARY FORCE? ..... *Yes.*

John Mumford (Signature of Man).
(Signature of Witness).

John Mumford's signing-on papers for the Canadian Overseas Expeditionary Force. He, like Flora's brother Edwin, was an Englishman who joined up in Ontario. Unlike him, he survived the war—his discharge record shows 'gunshot wound left foot.'

Part of 'Tin Town,' situated on the Portsmouth Road at Bramshott Common, taken about 1917. 'Postie' Louise Woods would cycle here on her round from Liphook.

Pictures of Flora in the Post Office house at Liphook – on back page of the Daily Mirror Thursday March 3rd, 1921, after *Bog Myrtle & Peat* was published.

WOMAN OF LETTERS.

VILLAGE POSTMISTRESS POETESS.

HER FIRST VOLUME.

From Our Own Correspondent.

LIPHOOK (Hants), Tuesday.

The people of Liphook have always believed that in the pleasant situation of their village, and the natural beauties of their countryside, they had enough for proper local pride. Now they find that they possess a hitherto undiscovered and unsuspected poetess.

She was already sufficiently well known to be something of a public figure, for the poetess is the postmistress, Mrs. Flora Thompson, whose first collection of poems is published by Philip Allan and Co., of London, this week, under the title, "Bog Myrtle and Peat." An advance copy shows it to be a slim volume of considerable merit, and it is being looked for with a good deal of interest locally.

Mrs. Thompson is a busy mother and housewife, as well as postmistress and poet.

"I started writing little things long ago," she told me to-day. "No one helped me, and I have carried on my passion for literature quite alone. In fact, I sometimes think I must be the most isolated of women who write poetry.

"The papers have published a few of my verses, and a year ago I sent some poems to Mr. Allan. He wrote an encouraging letter, and I have tried again, and this time the book is being published.

RATHER AUTOBIOGRAPHICAL.

"I work at my writing when my other housework is done, and how I have found time to do it is a long story. At present I have got a novel in hand. Of course, the central subject is a girl, and it is rather autobiographical.

"It is almost impossible for one to get away from oneself," she added artlessly.

Mrs. Thompson's poems are well written and show much promise. They bear traces of her having laboriously built up her technique upon the models of the greater poets. The volume opens with some lines to "Ronald Campbell Macfie:—

Yours are the moors, the billowy seas,
Tall mountains and blue distances.
Mine is a cottage garden, set
With marigold and mignonette,
And all the winding things that dare,
Without a gardener's fostering care.
Yet very well-content I rest
In my obscure perfumeless nest:
For from my cottage garden I
Can see your cloud-peaks pierce the sky.

"I am generally too busy in the mornings to write," said the postmistress, "but I make use of my ideas later. I have written lots of short stories and find time for a good deal of reading. Francis Thompson and Robert Browning are my favourites, but I don't like Swinburne."

The publishers had no idea as to what sort of a person Mrs. Thompson was, and her work has been taken entirely on its merits.

Article in *Daily Chronicle*, Wednesday March 2, 1921.

CONDUCTED BY FLORA THOMPSON.

CATHOLIC POETS OF THE NINETEENTH CENTURY.

I.—COVENTRY PATMORE.

DOWN to Elizabethan times all English poetry was Catholic poetry: Catholic, that is, in the full sense of having been written by Catholics for Catholics. The so-called Reformation, catastrophic misfortune as it proved to almost every other phase of the national life, might have been expected to cause a distinct cleavage in the spirit of national song. No such cleavage can be traced in it. Shakespeare's outward profession of faith is unknown; but many allusions in his works show that his sympathies, at least, were with the Old Religion. Other poets of the time were either sympathetic or indifferent; there is scarcely any trace in their works of the great upheaval in their midst; but they sang, as the true poet must always do, straight from the heart, and the heart of England was still essentially Catholic.

Fireside Reading Circle March 7, 1925:— Coventry Patmore was one of the poets whose work was introduced to Flora in Grayshott by Annie Symonds.

By FLORA THOMPSON.

JULY.

The seeded dandelion dim
Casts loose its air-globe on the breeze;
Along the grass the swallows skim;
The cattle couch among the trees.

Down waves successive of the year
We drop; but drop once more to rise,
With ampler view, as on we steer,
O! lovelier lights and loftier skies."

DURING the fourteen years I lived in a large seaside town I seldom saw the country in July or August, having a mistaken idea that for those two months it was, according to the slang of the day, "impossible," being parched, dust-laden, and wholly given over to charabanc trippers.

Peverel Paper July 18, 1925:— Flora notes here that she lived in Bournemouth for fourteen years before moving to Liphook.

Flora wrote for the *Catholic Fireside* for several years— alternating 'Peverel Paper' and 'Fireside Reading Circle' articles each fortnight.

'The Peverel Monthly' was distributed to members of 'The Peverel Society'– a postal writers' circle.

This June 1928 edition contains a chapter of Flora's own unpublished novel 'Gates of Eden'.

THE PEVEREL MONTHLY.

Edited by FLORA THOMPSON.

Vol I.	JUNE, 1928.	No. 6.

GATES OF EDEN. By FLORA THOMPSON.

Author of "Bog-Myrtle and Peat," "The Peverel Papers," etc.

CHAPTER II.

Mrs. Verlander sat at the tea-table and cut bread and jam into fingers for little Edmund. The sunset light, falling in one long ray between the window-frame and the drawn blind, showed her face, usually so dark and glowing, the colour of putty; there was swollen red about her eyes, and her lips were pressed into a thin line.

"Just one more peck, my duck!" she urged as she held the finger of food to the child's mouth. He bit at it obediently, but at every mouthful she had to coax him again, and, gradually, her strained features relaxed into tenderness.

The sunset ray fell upon the dark head of the mother and flushed the fair, delicate face of the child. Berengaria, entering noiselessly, thought of the scripture pictures in the lesson books at school. Neither of them noticed her, and she stood for a few moments watching them from the porch while she tried to still her quick breathing and trembling limbs.

'Woolmer Gate' in Griggs Green, Liphook — here seen extended
since the time the Thompsons bought it in July 1926

PROPERTY FOR SALE.

Rock Bottom £725   Price Freehold   £750.

Situation of Property "Woolmer Gate" Liphook.   Price Leasehold

ACCOMMODATION	Reception Rooms 2	Size of Drawing Room	Billiard Room
	Bedrooms 3	Size of Dining Room	Morning Room
Number of Floors	Bathrooms 1	Size of Principal Bedrooms	
	Dressing Rooms		
	Offices Kt-Sc&P.	Stabling: No. of Stalls	No. of Loose Boxes
	Coach House	Garage Room for one	

Style of Property Brick & tiled.   Aspect _____   Lighting _____

Soil _____   Drainage Modern cesspool.   Water Supply Pump

Distance Station 1½ mls Town ____ Church ____ Post Office ____ Golf Links ____
(Sea or River)

Extent of Grounds (or Garden) and Description Frontage 60 ft. Depth 250ft. more available.

Conservatories and Outbuildings _____

Freehold, Leasehold, or Copyhold ____ No. Years Leasehold ____ Ground Rent ____ Land Tax ____ Tithe ____

When Vacant _____   Rental Value _____

Fixtures to be taken over _____

Name and Address of Freeholder or Leaseholder ____ Mr Thompson

Instructed by E. B. & Son Submitting to Auction

Name and Address of Ground Landlord 7.7.28

Keys obtained at _____

Order to View on _____ Mrs. Thompson.

REMARKS:

Dated 8-9-27 _____   Board No. _____   Folio (or Reference) No. _____

Sale details of 'Woolmer Gate' in 1927/28

Sandy tracks through heather and birch on Weavers Down, near Liphook
— to Flora, this was 'Peverel Down,' and much of the writing in her
'Peverel Papers' relates to this area.

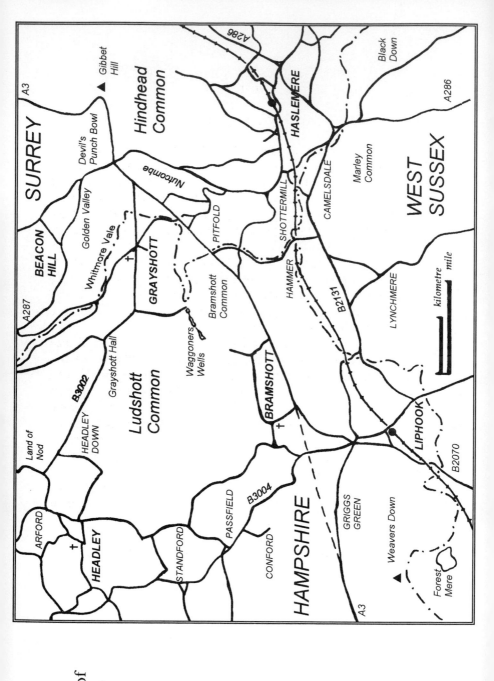

General map of
the Grayshott,
Haslemere,
Headley and
Liphook area

'Edmund'

During the time that Flora was at Grayshott, Britain became involved in the Boer War in South Africa. She tells us of opinions voiced in the village for and against the Boers, citing Walter Chapman's brother Ernest as a 'pro-Boer,' and Walter himself as one of the majority who supported the British action. Her concern was more personal, since her favourite brother Edwin, whom she refers to as 'Edmund' in her books, was fighting over there. She tells us how she travelled one day to Aldershot by train to see him off, and later lay awake at nights worrying about how he was getting on, and looking with concern at the list of casualties which she had to post in the office window each Sunday morning.

Edwin survived that conflict, only to perish some fifteen years later in the First World War. By this time Flora had two children of her own—Henry Basil had been born on 6th Oct 1909, six years after Winifred. The children were ill with whooping cough at the time of Edwin's last leave in Oxfordshire, and Flora had been unable to travel from Bournemouth to see him. Then three weeks later, on a glorious April morning in 1916 she tells us, a letter she had written to him was returned to her, marked in pencil, 'Killed in Action.'

Winifred has said of her mother's reaction to the news, that she was 'quite simply heart-broken.' Flora tells us she later reconciled herself to the fact that at least 'he had not relinquished life before he had well tasted it.' 'He went the way of the old heroes of his childhood,' she says, 'in the prime of his manhood, fighting for a cause he wholeheartedly believed in, and went swiftly and suddenly in the heat of the battle, a happy warrior.'

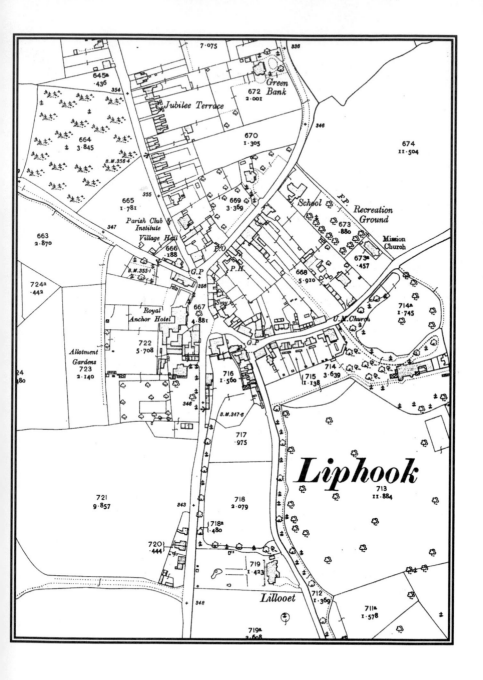

Centre of Liphook about 1909

To Liphook

Four months after Edwin's death, Flora returned to east Hampshire. As she explains, 'the return was not of her own seeking, but due to her husband's appointment as postmaster in the Heatherley district, an appointment which might have been to any other place of the same size in the south of England. But although she had had no choice in the matter, the prospect of visiting her old haunts was a pleasing one.' John Thompson had applied for the job of sub-postmaster at Liphook, just three miles from Grayshott, and he, Flora and the two children moved into the house next door to Liphook post office in August 1916. Fate had brought Flora back close to 'Heatherley,' and this time she was to stay for twelve years.

The *Guide to Liphook* published in 1925 begins:—

'The Hampshire village of Liphook stands upon the London to Portsmouth road at the juncture of three counties, Hampshire, Surrey and Sussex; 44 miles from London on the one hand and 25 from Portsmouth on the other. The railway station is upon the Portsmouth main line, therefore the train service is frequent and good, the entire journey from Waterloo to Liphook occupying 1 hour 40 minutes.'

In it, the publisher tells us that he 'desires to gratefully acknowledge his indebtedness to Mrs. Flora Thompson, author of "Bog Myrtle and Peat," "The Peverel Papers," etc., for the splendid descriptions of this charming part of England.'

Flora writes that Liphook 'combines within itself the moorland pine and heather of Hampshire; the leafy vales, deep lanes and sparkling watercourses of Surrey; and the turf and thyme-scented chalk downs of Sussex.' In spring, 'every path is a primrose path and every wood a bluebell wood;' in early summer there is the 'purple pageant of the heather upon the hills around; and that, in its turn, is succeeded by the gold and russet and crimson of autumn.'

In one of her *Peverel Papers* written while she w ̀s in Liphook, Flora mentions that 'the finest blackberries I have ever seen grow upon a heath about two miles from here. A much-frequented main road from London to the sea cuts through it, and motorists, halting for a picnic lunch, marvel at the exceptional size of the blackberries there. It is no wonder, really, for those particular bushes had a costly pruning: it took a European war to bring them to their present perfection.'

In the *Guide* she tells us that 'close by are the deserted sand-heaps and heathland where a camp which was in itself a large and populous town sprang up, served its purpose, and has almost disappeared.'

This was the camp built on Bramshott Common at the start of the First World War and which, by 1916 when she arrived, was used for the purposes of training newly-drafted Canadian soldiers before they were sent to the front. Consisting of many wooden huts, it was described by one regiment at the time as 'well-appointed, with good bathing and fumigating arrange-ments.' It spread out on either side of the main Portsmouth road, close to the old *Seven Thorns Inn* and next door to a 630-bed military hospital which had also been built there. Beside the road 'a straggle of corrugated-iron huts' grew up, referred to locally as 'Tin Town,' housing shops, cafés, churches, the bank and a post office *(see p. 73)*.

When Flora came it was very busy. She says in one of her *Peverel Papers* that 'tens of thousands of Canadian soldiers sojourned there—one contingent after another arrived, the men often soaked with rain or moiled with heat, and always cramped from the close quarters of wartime transport. They were drilled upon those open spaces so flattened by feet that even now the heather has scarcely begun to grow again.' Then, as she says, 'each battalion in its turn passed singing along that same main road to its fate.' The road they marched along, from camp to railway station, passed right by the post office door, and Flora's heart must have gone out to them as she remembered the recent loss of her brother. He had also been in a Canadian regiment.

But there was little enough time in the day for her to dwell on such things. The post office was under-staffed due to the men having been called up, and over-worked due to the presence of two large army camps in the district. Flora found herself getting up at four o'clock each morning to sort mail for four hours, before preparing the family breakfast and then sending the children off to school. After that there was shopping to do, with wartime queuing and rationing in force, and all on very little money.

'Postie'

🌀🌀🌀

Louise ("Louie") Woods was one of a staff of nine at Liphook at the time, and had joined at the age of nineteen in the same year that the Thompsons arrived. She remembers her day beginning at a quarter to six, arriving at the post office to find her letters for the morning delivery already sorted for her by Flora. She wore a uniform of which she says she was very proud, consisting of a three-quarter length dark blue jacket and skirt to match, with red piping, a boater with a gold-coloured G.P.O. badge, and the number five displayed on the lapels of her coat *(see p. 72)*.

After inspection by John Thompson, she would leave to deliver her morning round on a bicycle which she had bought from another postman for thirty shillings on joining. They had to provide their own 'dependable conveyance' for deliveries in those days. The round took her for about twenty miles through the country lanes of Hampshire and Sussex to such picturesque places as Milland, Iping, Conford and Waggoners Wells. At one cottage, she says, a woman would welcome her every day with a cup of tea, but post office regulations would not allow her to enter the door, nor remove the post bag from her back.

On another occasion a lady asked her to take a parcel to the office. Louie politely explained that as she was on her outward journey and already had a full load, she was not able to carry it for sixteen miles. The lady immediately put in a report to John Thompson, and on arriving back from her round, Louie found a note from him on the sorting desk reading, "Kindly state why you refused to take Mrs C's parcel," and she had to write an official apology.

The second delivery began at a quarter to four—this proved the hardest, especially in winter on unmade tracks through dark woods. She would often get a puncture riding over the rough ground and then, arriving back at the post office late, was met by a barrage of questions as to where she had been. They seldom believed her explanation, she says, but Flora was always at hand to console her by making her a cup of coffee. This was despite the fact that Louie did not drink coffee, but being young and shy she did not dare mention it to her employer's wife, and instead poured it surreptitiously into the pot plants so as not to offend her. No wonder Flora was surprised when her plants withered and died, she added.

Louie was nicknamed 'Postie' by the Canadian troops, and we are told that whenever she received a letter from a soldier, Flora would put it at the top of the pile she was sorting for her. One soldier Louie remembered in particular, according to her daughter, was a Sergeant John Mumford. Like several other men serving with Canadian regiments, including Flora's brother Edwin, John Mumford was an Englishman by birth, born in Southend-on-Sea. He had enlisted at Sarnia, Ontario, in January 1915 at the age of twenty-two, but did not arrive in England until 25th January 1917 when he was 'taken on strength' with the 9th Reserve Battalion at Bramshott. He then served in France from November 1917 with the 31st Battalion, and was wounded twice, in May and August of 1918—his record states 'gunshot wound left foot'—returning to Bramshott for treatment both times. Several opportunities, it would seem, for Louie to get to know him.

Happily his war, unlike that of so many of his comrades, ended without further loss or injury. His papers show that he 'ceased to be attached to the army' just before Christmas 1918 and was discharged in London, Ontario on 11th February 1919. Whether he wrote to Louie afterwards we do not know—none of her personal correspondence survives.

Post-war Pilgrimage

ᘒᘒᘒ

Flora tells us that, once settled at Liphook, she 'took the earliest opportunity of walking over the heaths and through the woods' to visit Grayshott. In her book *Heatherley* she calls this a 'post-war pilgrimage,' so dating it as after 1918. She says she 'found the village little changed in appearance,' and that 'the two short streets looked much as they had done,' perhaps 'a little dustier and shabbier as to paint,' and 'with new names over many of the shop fronts.' That afternoon she 'walked among the old familiar scenes like a ghost of the past.' Very few people were in the streets, and of those few she says none knew or recognised her.

Then, as she turned a corner, she saw 'coming towards her the reporter of a local newspaper and thought, "Ah, it's Tuesday!"' remembering that Tuesday had been his day in the past for collecting from Grayshott 'such scraps as the place afforded.' 'He was,' she said, 'evidently engaged in the same pursuit for he was walking, notebook in hand, in close converse with the village policeman.'

This reporter had been one of her friends in Grayshott, and she tells us that 'there had been a time when he would even have risked losing an item of news for the sake of a talk with her.' She remembered some of their shared experiences in the past, such as tramping over the moors and having stewed whortle-berries and cream for tea at a wayside inn. But that day he was scribbling in his notebook, and she says he did not look up as she passed by—nor, it seems, did she feel a sufficient urge to stop and wait for a while in order to renew his acquaintance.

She learned afterwards that he had served four years with the fighting forces in France, and had since married and had children. These experiences, she noted, 'had had little effect upon his outward appearance. He had still the same sturdy figure, bright inquisitive eyes and head bent a little forward as though perpetually in search of news.'

Flora tells us that they had once shared 'a rather gruesome experience' when, 'after sitting side by side on the top bar of a sluice at the lakes laughing and talking for an hour one summer evening they had learned the next day that, immediately after they left, the body of a drowned man had been taken from the water.'

In its issue of Saturday 12th May 1900, the *Haslemere Herald* carried a report, presumably written by her friend, which begins: 'There is an element of mystery surrounding the death of a labourer named Albert Pannell, aged 35, whose body last week was found in Waggoners Wells....'

The reporter was almost certainly William Austen Sillick, who at the age of twenty-one was the sole local representative for the *Haslemere Herald* during the time that Flora was in Grayshott *(see p.69)*.

According to an article published by that paper in 1948, to mark fifty years of his employment with them, he 'grew in wisdom and stature (sideways rather than up) and weekly travelled his wide district finding out the news and all the news and nothing but the news.' They added that 'he often came away with a piquant story which he loved to retell with far louder laughs from the teller than from the hearers.'

William Sillick was also an enthusiastic compiler of notes on the eminent people of the area. In Haslemere Museum, there is a lovingly gathered collection of newspaper cuttings and jottings of his, and a notebook in which he recorded information specifically about the personalities who lived in and around Grayshott.

How ironic, then, that it includes no mention of the young girl he had walked with on the heaths, and sat with for hours by Waggoners Wells. But how could he have known then that, one day, she also would be worthy of a place in his collection?

The Latecomer

Flora recalls that 'one of her first callers' when she arrived in Liphook was her old landlady from Grayshott days, 'Mrs Parkhurst.' It was, she says, 'a more cheerful, comfortable-looking and a much better-dressed Mrs Parkhurst than the one she remembered, but otherwise little changed.' When she had formerly known her 'she had looked older than her years, but the time between then and their second meeting had adjusted that matter and at sixty-five she looked much as she had at forty-five.' Flora tells us that 'Mrs Parkhurst had brought with her an intelligent-looking, smartly-dressed girl of twenty whom she introduced as "My youngest daughter, Elsie; the one you saw last as a tiny long-clothed baby in bed."' This had been her 'latecomer,' born to her when she had thought she was past child-bearing.

The fact that Flora more than once quotes a period of twenty years between her times at Grayshott and Liphook seems at first a mystery. The years of her likely departure from the area and of her return must have been etched in her mind—the year Queen Victoria died on the one hand and the year her brother died on the other—fifteen years apart. But in all probability twenty years passed before she felt free to follow her own pursuits after arriving in Liphook. This is borne out when we are told that 'Mrs Parkhurst had come by bus,' for Flora herself, in one of her *Peverel Papers*, says that 'buses here are a recent institution,' and this was written in 1924.

'Mrs Parkhurst' would therefore have seen Flora's own 'latecomer' when she visited her. Peter Redmond had been born to Flora when she was forty-one, on 19th October 1918, at the height of the 'flu epidemic which was then sweeping Europe and killing thousands who had otherwise survived the First World War. In that very month, ninety Canadian soldiers alone were buried in Bramshott churchyard, victims of the disease. Despite this, Louie Woods remembers the birth as a 'joyous occasion,' and recalls being allowed by John Thompson to see the baby and congratulate Flora.

The choice of Redmond as his second name has been seen by some as indicating that Flora, and perhaps more particularly John, supported the cause of John Redmond, the Irish nationalist who died in that year. Others see the name as a device contrived by Flora to commemorate her brother Edwin, whom she invariably referred to as Edmund in her books—so to her, the new baby may well have been Peter Edmund.

John Thompson

Louie Woods remembered John Thompson as a small, portly, well-dressed man with brown, wavy hair. He expected everyone to be as immaculately dressed as himself, with clean, neatly pressed uniform and shining brass buttons. He had a domineering personality and strong views, with the bearing and manner of a Sergeant major. Everyone, she said, was in awe of him. In the evening she might be talking to fellow postman Harry Envis while they stamped letters by hand in the sorting office, but as soon as they heard footsteps approaching from the postmaster's office adjoining, 'the door of which was always left open so he could overhear any forbidden conversations,' they would hastily part company, Harry pretending to hang up his coat or mail bag, and Louie busying herself stamping the letters.

Eileen Leggett (now Mrs Hobson), who worked there as a telephonist from the mid-1920s, says that he was 'very aloof and not popular among the postal staff; he was fair but very strict.' Her elder brother Joe Leggett describes him as 'a medium sized, neatly dressed man who appeared to have a sharp, authoritative voice and a finger on every pulse that made the postal service run smoothly.' He also tells the following story: 'At the age of eight in 1916, I was interested to see what our new postmaster looked like and found an excuse to enter the post office to get a glimpse of him. It was some kind of poor excuse, and when I was asked what I wanted, I learned very quickly from Mr Thompson that the post office was not a place for little lads to spend their time.'

He continues, 'I recall how in later years, I made my first withdrawal from my savings book, and with the patience of a schoolmaster, he handed me form after form until at last I made it out correctly and received the two shillings I'd applied for. Everything with him had to be correct and on time. That withdrawal was a lesson to me, and whenever I went to the post office to renew vehicle licences, I made sure the forms were properly made out and signed. As postmaster, he spent a lot of time in the office making certain that the incoming and outgoing mail was received and dispatched on time. His observation and supervision was somewhat irksome to the postal staff, but they had great respect for his fairness towards them and his devotion to the post office.'

John Thompson's favourite relaxation was fishing. In his off-duty hours he would go with Harry Envis and others to Waggoners Wells or one of the other many ponds and lakes around Liphook. Joe Leggett remembers that 'the only time I ever saw him out of the office would be on his bicycle to or from Forest Mere, where he spent his leisure time with rod and line by the lake. I and other boys used to swim in that lake, and many of us experienced the rough edge of his tongue if we happened to swim near to where he was patiently watching for his float to be jerked by perch or to be drawn under by tench. Nevertheless, as village lads, we had no hate campaign against him.'

Did John Thompson dominate his wife? Was he the 'dodder person' in her life? Eileen Leggett, talking of the time when they were next-door neighbours at Griggs Green in 1926, said: 'We knew nothing of her being a writer, but my mother, a keen judge of character, soon decided that Mrs Thompson was a "lady" but her husband "no gentleman." People think she was intimidated by him but, at least by the time I knew them, in her gentle way she managed him nicely.'

And even at an earlier period, immediately after the First World War, as Louie Woods recalled, 'despite her husband's overbearing personality, this did not deter Flora from her writings. She would shut herself away, in her own sparsely furnished room which consisted only of a writing desk, two chairs and a waste paper basket, writing her essays and poetry. Her husband seldom entered, and the children were forbidden to interrupt her whilst writing.'

'The Postmistress Poet'

Louie tells us that she frequently visited Flora in her study and was presented one day with a book of her poetry entitled *Bog Myrtle and Peat*, published in 1921, but she says she was not sufficiently interested in its contents herself, and passed it on for her mother to enjoy. The *Daily Chronicle* of Wednesday, March 2nd 1921 reported on the book under the headline 'Woman of Letters,' and the *Daily Mirror* of the following day showed on its back page two photographs of her at work *(see p.74)*. Her daughter Winifred remembers that John and the rest of the family were rather amused by it all.

The inspiration to persevere with her poetry had come primarily, it is thought, from her friendship with Dr Ronald Campbell Macfie, whom she had first met in 1912 after she had won a competition to write a criticism on his ode about the sinking of the *Titanic*. Up to that time she had entered and had won some writing competitions in *The Ladies' Companion*, and she went on to sell other prose articles and a number of mainly romantic short stories during her time at Liphook, but fired by Macfie, we are told she longed above all to see herself as a poet.

It was not to be. *Bog Myrtle and Peat* was not a commercial success, and Flora turned her energies to other forms of writing.

She told reporters at the time that she was also working on a novel. 'Of course, the central subject is a girl, and it is rather autobiographical,' she said. As far as we know, she never did attempt to write a novel on the theme of *Dodder*, so perhaps she was referring to *Gates of Eden*, which she is known to have completed in draft form, most probably while she was at Liphook. An edited and serialised version of it appeared in *The Peverel Monthly*, the internal magazine of her postal writers circle, but the novel has never yet been published as an entity. In it we are told the tale of a young girl named Berengaria who seems to have all the traits of Flora—a love of the countryside, a father who was a stone mason, a mother finding it hard to make ends meet and, inevitably, a younger brother named Edmund. While clearly fiction, it is perhaps more revealing about the true character of Flora herself than are her more famous works which are generally classified as non-fiction.

Interestingly, two earlier attempts at much the same story, then called *The Stithy*, have also been found, and in these Flora writes using the 'first-person' viewpoint of the heroine. In *Gates of Eden*, however, she settles for the more disinterested 'third-person' viewpoint—and this has since become familiar to us as the style she later used in *Lark Rise*.

Bog Myrtle (Sweet Gale*)—Myrica gale*

Alternative names: Golden Withy, Flea-Wood, & others.
A useful as well as a sweetly resinous shrub. It provided faggots for the cloam oven, it kept fleas away, and Highlanders slept on flea-proof beds of the Bog Myrtle, it was put to good use to repel moths, it gave a yellow dye; and more important, it was one of those plants which gave a flavouring to ale or beer before the popularisation of hops ….

Bog Myrtle must have been much more common before the reclamation of wet land, the draining of the Fens, etc. Where it is locally dominant, for instance in parts of the wet, sandy basin of the New Forest, it sends out a delicious fragrance, especially in the flowering months of April and May.

from 'The Englishman's Flora' by Geoffrey Grigson

Nature Notes

Flora's move towards, not only the style, but also the content of *Lark Rise* seems to have evolved considerably during her time at Liphook. It was here that she started writing nature articles for *The Catholic Fireside* magazine, and noted that 'the feature most liked in the articles were sketches of old country life and characters remembered from my childhood, and I determined that at some future time I would describe them more fully.'

She called her nature notes *The Peverel Papers*, and later, when she started her postal writers circle this was known as *The Peverel Society*. Nobody is quite sure how the word Peverel came to her, although it has been suggested that perhaps one of her jobs in the 1897/98 period, between leaving Fringford and arriving at Grayshott, might well have been at Hatfield Peverel in Essex. This is close enough to Halstead, where she tells us she saw her first moving picture in 1898, and also to 'the Essex saltmarsh, bluish-mauve with sea lavender, and a tidal river with red fisher sails upon it' which she says she also saw during that time. Could there have been some memory from her time in Essex which she wished to keep alive in Hampshire?

Whatever her past, we know that in Liphook at least she associated the name Peverel with one of her favourite haunts, Weavers Down. This is described by her in the *Guide to Liphook* as 'a land of warm sands, of pine and heather and low-lying boglands; a stretching moor through which a spur of the South Downs, terminating in the little rounded hill rising like a miniature mountain on the Liphook side, runs like a backbone.'

She spent long afternoons walking with her little brown dog, Prince, in the countryside around and beyond Liphook. 'Nineteen or twenty miles was nothing to her,' as one villager put it. Flora herself tells of following an old packhorse track for miles into Sussex one day, 'quite forgetting that I had to retrace my steps some time or other.' 'By a lucky chance,' she says, 'as it approached nightfall I found a shilling in my pocket and a railway station at hand to bring me back to the twentieth century.' One feels she would not be so lucky these days.

While she enjoyed many happy hours alone on her rambles, she also joined the Haslemere Natural History Society and most probably went with them on some of their regular local 'fungus forays.' She certainly records in a *Peverel Paper* of 'feasting royally' on fungi during 'the lean months following the armistice'—but she also says that she gave it up on hearing that the author of one of the learned reference books had himself 'experimented one time too many' with them. Her two-shilling annual membership of the Society is recorded (for Miss F Thompson) by Haslemere Museum in the years 1917, 18 and 1922 to 1927—in other words, every full year that she was in Liphook except for the three in which she was most probably occupied nursing Peter.

Joe Leggett remembers her coming upon him 'out of the blue' one day when he was in some dense shrubbery near Foley Gate, gazing into a nest to see if fledglings had hatched. 'She thought I was one of those boys that deliberately destroyed the nests,' he says, 'and I had to assure her that I knew of many nests which I observed but never disturbed. It was the first time I had heard her speak, and I was fascinated by the kind, authoritative quality of her voice and her easy flow of conversation.'

His sister Eileen remembers Flora taking a photograph of her riding one of the farm horses—'quite a good one it was too,' she says. Flora gave her the glass-plate negative to keep, but it had seemed nothing special to a sixteen year old girl, and over the years she lost it. 'I've kicked myself several times since then,' she says, 'but how were we to know then that Mrs Thompson would be famous one day?'

Flora tells us in her *Peverel Papers* of meeting others during her Liphook walks. One was the old shepherd who, she says, during the time when wartime lighting regulations were at their most stringent, pointed at the full moon saying, 'They can't put that out, nor the sun, nor the stars in all their mightiness.' She gives us several other tales from him, but Joe Leggett recalls that after the First World War his parents had made a dilapidated cottage of theirs habitable for an aged, ex-Southdown shepherd to live out his retirement, and that he 'attracted the attention of Mrs Thompson like a metal to a magnet, and the old shepherd simply fascinated her with his fantastic stories about his imaginary herd of sheep on Weavers Down.' He adds that 'it was very kind of Mrs Thompson to lend an ear to the old shepherd's imagination.'

Another real-life character she came across was Bill Tidy the knife-grinder and his wife Maggie, who lived out on Lynchmere Common for many years. Flora tells us: 'In the shelter of a circle of hollies, old trees almost as tall and bushy as oaks, a tinker and his wife had made their home for forty years. Inside the circle of the trees was a space as large as a cottage, thick foliage formed the roof and walls, and the floor was the natural earth, hardened by forty years' use. The little home was neatly arranged; there was room for the sleeping tent, for the kitchen part with its brick fireplace and pots and pans, and even a corner fenced off with hurdles and lined with straw for the donkey. Honeysuckle draped the door opening, and before it stretched nature's garden, miles wide, of heather, bracken and gorse. Every day the occupants went out with their knife-grinding apparatus and china-riveting outfit and earned enough to supply their needs—earned more, indeed, as it proved in the end, than was good for them.'

She goes on to tell us how, having had too much to drink, 'one night last June the little party went home, the donkey the only sensible being among them, or at any rate the only one of them who was never suspected of dropping the match which set fire to the place and left the holly roof and walls a ring of charred skeletons and the beds, tents and household goods within a heap of smouldering ruins.'

John Budd, a Liphook villager at the time, confirms the incident and says they were a 'strange old couple' who lived rough in a tent on Lynchmere Common. She went along the road singing out, "A'y old rahzors or scissors to grind, Mr Tidy's comin' be'ind," and he never got off his cart—just sat there pedalling his grindstone and sharpening cut-throat razors, knives, scissors and so on.' John Budd also tells us that, 'after the fire they just moved across the road and hung up a new piece of canvas under some big hollies by Danley Farm.' 'We children called the place "Holly Trees Villa,"' he says.

Australian Saga

When the Thompsons first arrived at Liphook in 1916, their daughter Winifred was twelve, and their son Basil six. Louie Woods remarked that 'Winifred took after her mother, but was noted for her independent character—she detested her Christian name and insisted on being called Diana, though her mother called her Di for short.' Basil, she said, 'was determined, like his father, and even at the early age of eight he already had the inclination to emigrate to Australia.'

Winifred, or Diana as we shall now call her, went to a private school in Haslemere according to other biographers, but no records now exist as to which one. When she left, she started working for her father as a telephone operator at Liphook post office. Here she met and became close friends with Cecil Cluer, a local boy about eighteen months younger than herself, who had started work at the post office as a telegram boy when he was fourteen, then moved on to Haslemere as a van driver. He lived in Bramshott, and eventually he and Diana became engaged.

We believe that Basil went to Churchers College in Petersfield in September 1922—no official admission records exist, but the school magazine records welcoming a B. Thomson *(sic)* in that month. Ron Chappell, a friend of Joe Leggett's, remembers that there was always rivalry between boys from the local village school where he went and those from Churchers. He and a friend had met Basil and a friend in Tower Road once and thrown a blackbird's egg at him—it had hit him on the chin and dripped all down his uniform. Basil ran home crying, he says, and John Thompson came to see his father about it. Apparently the fathers 'laughed it off.'

Basil was obviously on friendly terms with Diana's fiancé Cecil, and they decided to travel together to the banana plantation of Flora's brother Frank in Queensland, with the idea of making some money. They left England in February 1926 when Basil was still only sixteen. Cecil was not quite twenty-one at the time, and his sister Phyllis remembers 'as if it was yesterday' her father giving consent for him to go abroad, saying that as he was set on it he might just as well sign the paper.

It is not clear whether Cecil intended to return and live in England, or wanted to make a home for Diana over there, but as it turned out neither happened, for although Basil returned in 1928, Cecil never did, and his engagement to Diana ended. His sister says that Diana wrote to him asking if she might break it off, and this most probably at the instigation of John and Flora who 'didn't think the match was good enough.' Cecil, she says, wrote home telling them not to fuss or blame Diana for it.

Eileen Leggett, who worked with Diana at the time, remembers that she took her opal engagement ring off only after Basil had come back, as if he had brought the news to her of the engagement being ended. 'She seemed distressed then,' says Eileen, 'but we never talked about it.'

To Griggs Green

୧ଇ ୧ଇ ୧ଇ

It was during this time that Flora finally achieved her dream of owning rather than renting a house. The lack of a night-time operator at Liphook telephone exchange had meant that the Thompsons had had to live next to the post office ever since their arrival in the village, but in July 1926, nearly ten years after their arrival, the problem was apparently resolved and, taking out a mortgage of £675, they bought *Woolmer Gate*, a newly-built three-bedroomed house at Griggs Green, about 1½ miles away. It was also close to Flora's cherished Weavers Down.

Their neighbours here were Mr & Mrs Leggett, two of whose six children, Joe and Eileen, we have already mentioned. They had a small farm at Grove House next door to the Thompsons, and a larger one close by (at Hartley Farm, now under the Old Thorns golf course). Eileen, their youngest who was sixteen at the time, remembers that when the Thompsons first came to live there, Flora was in a fairly sad frame of mind owing to the recent departure of Basil to Australia. But she adds, 'as time passed and news of his safe arrival reached her, she began to look more cheerful.'

There was much movement of livestock going on, but despite this she 'couldn't remember them ever complaining of the farm activities, though we must have been very noisy with the necessary work with the animals in the early hours.' In fact, she says, 'Mrs Thompson found it all of great interest.' She describes Flora as 'a lovely neighbour; she was unobtrusive, yet one could turn to her for advice, as I often did. I used to visit her every Thursday afternoon for a cosy chat and to listen to their "wireless," which they had just acquired and were very enthusiastic about. I always left before four o'clock, so that she could listen to Choral Evensong, which she loved—though I don't remember her being a churchgoer.' The Leggetts were Roman Catholics, and Eileen says that Flora 'was very interested in the Catholic church,' but felt that they ought not to have been so much in awe of their priest, Father Atherton, who used to look them up and want explanations if they missed church or Sunday School.

Eileen had a special reason to be grateful to Flora. 'She decided there was no future for me working on the farm,' she tells us, 'yet there were few other openings in a little village like Liphook, whose population was then about 3,000 for the whole parish, so she suggested that I should apply for the post of part-time operator at the telephone exchange. I know I would not have been Mr Thompson's choice—but she arranged for me to get the appointment. So started two years or more of close association with Flora Thompson and her daughter.'

The Leggett's son Joe was the one who at the age of eight had found an excuse to enter the post office to get a glimpse of the new Postmaster, and who Flora had later disturbed while he was out birdnesting. He says he was glad that by the time they became neighbours he had 'probably grown beyond recognition'! He tells us that Flora became a regular customer at their door for dairy produce, but that 'although she came every day, there was little conversation apart from the usual pleasantries and comment about the weather. She was neatly dressed in good quality clothing appropriate to the time of year and suitable for her walks in the wildest parts of the surrounding district.'

'I can recall,' he says, 'how in inclement weather she would appear in a very smart blue Burberry raincoat, a waterproof hat of the same material and button-up footwear that reached well above the ankles. In better weather she usually wore skirt and blouse; nothing gaudy, but always in good taste.'

Eileen tells us that, until a night-time 'caretaker' could be recruited at the post office, John Thompson still had to leave the cottage every evening and cycle to the post office to take over night duty from Diana until the early morning, when the sorters arrived and combined the exchange duty with their sorting. She adds, 'I think this arrangement suited Mrs Thompson very well.'

Diana worked a permanent "split-duty" at the exchange—9am to 1pm and 4.30pm to 8pm. Eileen worked part-time at first, helping Diana from 9am to 12.30, then progressing to full-time later. Liphook had about a hundred subscribers in those days, and the operators knew most of them by name. 'It was a friendly little exchange,' Eileen tells us. 'People would say, "Give me the Green Dragon," or whatever, and if the number was engaged we would ring them back later when it was free.'

The split-shift arrangement allowed Diana time to go out walking with her mother in the afternoons. Eileen remembers that she frequently did this, and that mother and daughter were very close, rather like two sisters in their affection. Her brother Joe says 'they were so much alike that people felt sure they were sisters, because Flora carried her age so well.'

He also remembers meeting young Peter Thompson, then aged eight. 'I was harnessing our ex-army war veteran mule in the grounds of Grove House,' he says, 'and was being watched by Peter from his side of the fence. When I hitched the mule to the cart, Peter asked me where I was going. "Up to the farm on Weavers Down," I replied. He asked if he could come with me, and I suggested that he should ask his mother. He went indoors, but did not return straight away. As I left our premises, he and his mother were at their gate and he was trusted into my care. His mother asked me to let him see all the interesting things about the farm and remarked, "Now I can get on with the work in my study." I wondered at the time, but didn't ask, what sort of work it could be that she was doing.'

'During his school holidays he spent quite a lot of time with me,' says Joe. 'He was good company, and I found him to be very well-behaved, intelligent, cheerful and well spoken. He was devoted to his mother, father and sister, and also to the brother who was then in Australia. He was about four feet tall, plump in build, had a clear complexion and wore the grey uniform of a local private school. As with his brother and sister, his mother's features were strongly reflected in him.' Joe adds that, at about this period, the character 'Just William' was appearing in a magazine, and apart from William's round shoulders, untidy hair and devilment, Peter in his opinion somewhat resemble that particular character.

'Like his mother,' Joe tells us, 'he was also keen to look up in the rafters of derelict buildings for owls' nests, and I was puzzled sometimes when he said his mother and sister were going up to Peverel. I had no idea where Peverel was, but his words stayed in my mind to ring a bell many years later.'

It is interesting to note here that one story from Flora's time at Liphook was apparently recorded out of context by her in *Candleford Green* (see p.480 in the Penguin trilogy). 'The case of the man who had systematically stolen pigwash from a neighbour' happened at Griggs Green, according to Eileen Leggett who says that their family were actually the victims of this crime.

Farewell to 'Peverel'

The house at Griggs Green suited Flora wonderfully, but it seems that hardly had they settled there than John got itchy feet again. He saw in the Post Office Circular of 6th July 1927 a vacancy advertising the sub-postmaster's job at Dartmouth, to be filled by 6th November. The annual salary offered was £215, almost a 50% increase on the £145 he was then receiving. In addition it was by the sea and, being born on the Isle of Wight, he had always wanted to move back to the coast again. Applications had to be made within a week. He applied, and was successful, his appointment being noted in the Post Office Circular of 3rd August 1927.

An article in the *Haslemere Herald* of 12th November 1927, under the heading 'Presentation to Postmaster,' reported: 'An interesting ceremony took place on Thursday afternoon at Hewshott House, Bramshott, the residence of Capt B.D. Byfield, when a cheque for £40 and a list of subscribers was presented to Mr J.W. Thompson, the Postmaster of Liphook, who is leaving the district on his promotion to a similar position at Dartmouth, South Devon.' It added that they 'all wished to show their appreciation of Mr Thompson's work as postmaster during his eleven years' stay among them,' saying that they had 'always found him courteous, obliging and willing to help whenever possible.' Mr Thompson, it said, 'feelingly responded,' which is perhaps not surprising, since the sum of money he had just been given was quite considerable for those times.

Whether Flora also 'feelingly responded' to the prospect of having to move so soon away from her new house and from Hampshire we can only guess. *Woolmer Gate* was put on the market with a local estate agent at the beginning of September 1927, valued at £750, but did not sell. Eileen Leggett recalls that 'Mrs Thompson and Diana were quite happy to stay on at Griggs Green for however long it took to sell the house' while John Thompson started his job in Dartmouth. Other sources mention Flora planting masses of flowers in her garden during the spring of 1928, in order to make a 'defiant blaze of colour' in that last summer. Eventually the house seems to have been 'submitted to auction' in July 1928, with a 'rock bottom' price set at £725. Perhaps this did the trick—certainly by the end of the year they had moved out, on a day, we are told, when 'rain poured down from morning to night without ceasing.'

Eileen Leggett tells us, 'When they did leave they were sad to go, and Diana's first letters to me showed that they felt the wrench and didn't immediately like the change.' But obviously there were compensations, for eventually, she says, 'they soon began to enjoy it there.' And on a personal note she adds, 'I am glad that we knew Flora Thompson when she was not famous, nor did we dream that she was likely to be. We liked her for what she was, a very considerate and charming lady.'

Flora had written some seventy *Peverel Papers* over the six years between 1922 and 1927. These formed the bulk of her output while in Liphook, but she also had other work to her credit. During the same period she had, among other things,

Advertisement in *The Catholic Fireside*, December 1927

'ghosted' for another big-game hunter, conducted a monthly 'Fireside Reading Circle' for three years in *The Catholic Fireside*, started her own postal writers circle ('The Peverel Society'), and written the 1925 *Guide to Liphook*.

She was, by any measure, a busy and productive writer at this stage in her career—but she was still unknown to the world at large.

From Liphook to Dartmouth

The sub-postmaster's job at Liphook had become vacant in the Spring of 1916 when Mr J.M. Campbell was compulsorily retired. Post Office archives tell us that he was 'inefficient.'

The vacancy was advertised in the Post Office Circular of 30th May at a salary of £125 a year, stating that: *'The incoming postmaster will be required to occupy the official residence for which an annual rent will be charged at the rate of 14 per cent. of the salary. The accommodation comprises two sitting-rooms, four bedrooms and the usual offices, with a good garden. The Sub-Postmaster will also be required to provide for Telephone calls at night and on Sundays when the staff is not in attendance and for this duty remuneration will be made at the usual rates. With this exception the salary named constitutes the entire remuneration for all branches of duty.'*

John Thompson was anything but inefficient, as the subscribers to his parting testimonial demonstrate.

When he moved to Dartmouth in November 1927, he was succeeded at Liphook by Mr E. A. W. Gray, a Counter Clerk and Telegraphist in Eastern Central District Office, London, at £145 per annum. The salary increase during eleven years reflects the normal £5 p.a. increments at biennial periods offered to sub-postmasters at that level.

This move from Hampshire to Devon seems to have set a precedent, for when John Thompson finally retired in April 1935, it was the same Mr Gray who replaced him in Dartmouth.

Fame at the End

Although her *Peverel Papers* ceased after December 1927, Flora did not stop writing. She was, unconsciously of course, working towards the book which would make her name. In 1936 and in 1937 'The Lady' printed *The Tail-less Fox* and *Old Queenie*, articles written by Flora from her memories of poverty and childhood times. Their acceptance prompted her to offer two further essays, *An Oxfordshire Hamlet in the Eighties* and *May Day in the Eighties* to 'The National Review,' which published them in 1937 and 1938. From these successes, she determined to write a book based on the same ideas. This was *Lark Rise*, which she sent to Oxford University Press in 1938— it was accepted by them, published in March 1939, and became an almost immediate success.

Flora was by this time over sixty years old. She started work on the sequel, *Over to Candleford*, as the Second World War began, and struggled to complete the work by early 1941. It was another success, and she was urged to write on in the same style. But later that year, tragedy struck. Peter, who had joined the Merchant Navy, was lost when his ship went down in an Atlantic convoy in September.

Flora's 'Peverel Society' had continued for fourteen years since leaving Liphook, but now in 1941 she wound it up. With considerable effort, although her health was deteriorating, she started on a further sequel in the Spring of 1942, and completed *Over to Candleford*, which was published in January 1943. She then wrote a fourth part, *Heatherley*, taking the story of 'Laura' further to Grayshott, but although completed she never submitted this for publication. Instead she worked on what was to be her last book, *Still Glides the Stream*, which she finished in August 1946—it was published posthumously.

She died in bed at her home on the evening of 21st May 1947, while John was downstairs having taken her a cup of tea just half an hour before. In a letter written a month later, John recalls how he 'felt stunned' when he went up and found her gone. He survived her by not much more than a year.

• • •

Perhaps, after all, the dodder could not live without the heather.

*John and Flora's signatures
on the Mortgage document
for 'Woolmer Gate,'
dated 2nd July 1926*

From the Archives

༄ ༄ ༄

CONTENTS

From the Archives

In September 1996, Gillian Lindsay (author of the biography *Flora Thompson - The Story of the 'Lark Rise' Writer*) visited the Harry Ransom Humanities Research Center at the University of Texas in Austin to search the archives for any information which might have evaded previous researchers.

There she discovered a box of miscellaneous papers which, to her eyes, seemed to have remained untouched. There was no index of its contents, but on sifting through she found a number of items clearly relating to work in progress on *Heatherley*, including one whole chapter which had not been included in the final work as selected and published by Margaret Lane in 1979.

We have already mentioned a number of these items earlier— in particular the 'missing' chapter on the 'Jeromes'—and they are included here for your reference.

[Page numbers quoted refer to the OUP edition of *A Country Calendar* selected and edited by Margaret Lane.]

1. *Flora describes her ideas for chapters in* Heatherley

Flora wrote:—

'The following chapter is the story of the Hertfords and the climax which led to Laura finding a room for herself in the village.' *[VI. The Hertfords]*

'The next after that deals with her life as a bachelor girl in that room, together with an attempt to picture life in those days, fashions, ideas, prices, etc.' *[VII. Living alone and liking it]*

'Then descriptions of the various and varied people she met, including the old big-game hunter who formerly appeared in the earlier part of the book, of the outbreak of the Boer War and its effect on village life, and so on. The aim being a picture of life in those times as lived in a semi-suburban, semi-rural community.' *[This is not the structure finally used]*

2. *Draft version, part of 'VII. Living alone and liking it'*

[The final version in 'Heatherley' is very similar to this, but interestingly Flora there refers to her landlady as Mrs Parkhurst rather than, as here, Mrs Chivers.]

[see p.243] She heard no nightingale, but, while she was still standing there in the shadow of the trees, she heard approaching her on the road the soft, slithering sound of deflated bicycle tyres through the thick dust of the roadway. The ~~cyclist~~ bicycle came slowly into her view ~~and passed~~, still with that heavy, slithering sound, and she saw that ~~its rider~~, her invisible cyclist, was a sailor, an ordinary bell-bottomed blue jacket. His behaviour however was not at all ordinary for, leaning forward towards the handlebars, he was sobbing aloud. Sobbing broken-heartedly, he approached and passed her, unaware of her existence, and she herself, knowing nothing of the cause of his grief but with many conjectures, came out of her hiding place and took the road towards her home. She had gone out to hear the nightingales and over-heard instead the sound of human suffering and that ~~amidst the loveliest~~ at a time when our earth is at its freshest and gayest.

When Laura first went to live in her house her landlady, Mrs Chivers, was about forty-five, tall and massively built with dark hair and eyes and well-defined features. Occasionally, when some passing excitement had brought a faint flush to her sallow cheek and caused her ~~still~~ fine eyes to kindle, she might have still been thought a handsome woman, but constant child-bearing and the strain of bringing up a large family on insufficient means had lined her face, sharpened her voice, and destroyed the contours of her figure. In her person she was scrupulously clean and fairly tidy, though her dress was that of all over-worked, working-class mothers of the day, patched and faded old garments of nondescript hue, partly covered by a large white apron.

With seven children still living at home her life was indeed a hard one, washing and ironing and cleaning and cooking from morning to night for ten people. Even when more leisured housewives were enjoying their evening repose she was serving a hot meal to her husband and two sons who went out to work all day and had yet to pack their meals to the morrow, get her younger children to bed and do what was necessary for Laura. Sometimes when Laura ...

3. *Draft version, part of 'XI. Post-war Pilgrimage'*

[The final version in 'Heatherley' tells us nothing of 'Alma's' actions on the day, nor of 'Mr Hertford's' life in Broadmoor later, nor does it mention Conan Doyle by name, nor the name of Flora's dog, Prince.]

... a girl of her age might excusably have done, she walked firmly into the room where the murderer still hung over his victim, took the baby from out of its bath and carried it to safety. Afterwards of course she must have suffered from the shock, but, at the time, she behaved like a heroine. Good, steadfast little Alma!

Mr Hartford spent the rest of his life at Broadmoor. Laura often pictured him there, sitting with his head in his hands, as, according to the newspaper reports, he had done throughout his trial. But, even towards the wretched, time is merciful, and some time after she returned to live in the district, Laura learned from a relative of his who had visited him that he recovered his reason sufficiently to be allowed to work at his trade in the prison workshop. The relative then described him as a white-haired old man, harmless and tranquil, happy in his work, and still happier in that much that had passed had been wiped from his memory. He still had his delusions and one of these was that his wife came frequently to visit him. She, poor soul, was at rest.

[see p.304] By the time Laura re-visited Heatherley, "the awful affair at the post office" was an old story and Mrs Apsley did not dwell on it. The conversation turned to the time of Heatherley's prosperous days, ~~when Dr Conan Doyle lived~~, when trade was good in the shops, apartment houses were full, and famous men and women lived in the neighbourhood. The celebrities who lived in or near the village had long before Laura's visit died of gone away. Mrs Apsley said that she thought that one or two well-known people still lived on or round about the hill, but you didn't seem to hear so much as formerly about such people, the war, she supposed had altered ideas. Visitors still came to the hotels there, though more just to lunch or dine, than to make a long stay now that the motor car had brought the place within easy reach of London. A new class of visitor had appeared of late, brought there in crowds by the motor-coaches for a day's outing on the heathery hill and these, Mrs Apsley thought, had driven away what she called the better

106

class of visitor. She was quite tolerant of these new day-visitors for, when Laura mildly remarked that no doubt they enjoyed their outings, she said she did not begrudge them their pleasure, for they brought a little custom to the shops and their money was as good as anybody else's, though she did wish they would not strew the place with bottles and orange peel and paper bags. And, to show that she had forgiven Laura for criticising her soda rock cakes, she voluntarily brought a dish of water for her little dog. ~~Prince, who had been surreptitiously fed on rather dry cakes, lapped it up thankfully~~.

ೞ ೞ ೞ

4. *Attempt at starting a section*
—not used in the final book

Laura herself had an unpleasant experience of that kind. One summer day a stranger called at the office and in some way entered into conversation with her ...

Laura herself had one unpleasant experience of the kind. One summer day a middle-aged man who was a stranger to her called at the office and, by way of asking for some item of information about the district, entered into conversation with her ...

Laura herself had one unpleasant experience of the kind. One summer day a middle-aged man who was a stranger to her called at the post office. He was out cycling and was not sure of his way and when Laura had directed him, he remained for some little time, talking. His appearance and conversation were interesting. He was evidently a man of education and refinement and his personality appealed to Laura, less on account of his apparent refinement than because he was deformed, being very short of stature and almost a hunchback. She felt deep pity for him and when he asked for her name and address, saying that he would like to write to her, she gave it willingly. A few days later she received a letter from him enclosing a cheque which he begged her to accept in the spirit in which it was offered. She had said she had no bicycle and he would like her to have one and, it must be added, he gave as his reason that he would [like] her to meet him for rides together. That wish should have acted as a danger signal and no doubt it would had it come from a ordinary, normal man, but his affliction blinded Laura to possibilities of motive and though, of course, she returned his cheque, she refused to accept the offered bicycle as kindly as possible, and the correspondence continued.

He bore an old and romantic name and his home was many miles from Heatherley. During the next few weeks he called several times at the post office and was received by Laura with no misgivings, she liked him, and she also felt sorry for his affliction. On his part, it may at once be said, there were no evil intentions, he liked her, was, as it afterwards appeared, a little in love with her, though of this she did not dream.

He had asked her many times to tell him when she would be off duty, so that they could have a little walk and a talk together, but she never responded to this suggestion until one day he exclaimed: "But surely you are free on Sunday. What about next Sunday? Will you have tea with me at one of the hotels?" He mentioned the largest and most fashionable. Laura said no, she was afraid she could not, then, melted by his expression of disappointment, said: "Would you care to come to tea with me at my lodgings?" It was at once obvious that he would care to, very much, and so it was arranged. Mrs .... when asked for the loan of her front parlour for an hour was quite agreeable and when she was told the name and address of the expected guest she was pleased and interested. His home was not very far from her own in childhood and she knew the family of 'the gentleman' and her manner and remarks suggested that in her opinion Laura was to be highly honoured in entertaining such a distinguished guest.

Sunday came and tea was laid, with honey and cakes and a bunch of delphiniums, brought by Laura. The guest arrived, red-faced and panting, poor little manikin, after his long, uphill ride. On closer acquaintance he ...

• • •

[We have not been able to identify this cyclist, seemingly from the Selborne area. But it is interesting to note a comment in a booklet† written about Frank Patterson, the well-known cycling illustrator, that 'he and Flora Thompson were contemporaries, born within a few years of each other and both sharing a deep understanding of the country ways. It is just possible that during his cycle rides into the country from Wonersh, Patterson could have called into the post office at Grayshott and met Flora .... The result of a combining of talent would have been fantastic ... but it was never to be.'

† *'Frank Patterson' by Gerry Moore*]

5. *Another attempt which was not used in the final book*
[We have not been able to identify the Bohemian family]

"Bohemian" was a word on everybody's lips in those days. Like the old lady's Mesopotamia it was a blessed word, which could mean a good deal or a very little. An impromptu picnic or dance, reclining in a hammock within sight of passers by on the public road, informal manners, gay spirits, an easy, careless style of dress, especially if it included bright or what were known as artistic colours, were passed as Bohemian with many who knew not the whereabouts of that country or the habits of its inhabitants. Others, and those of the kind not to be trifled with, classed as Bohemian those they suspected of loose morals, of not paying their debts, or of being incompetent housekeepers. It could be applied to a couple living together without matrimony, or to a woman who, having a maid, herself opened her own front door to callers. Any departure from convention short of punishable crime was Bohemian.

There was in Heatherley at least one family of Bohemian repute. It consisted of two young couples living together in one house, in itself a more unusual arrangement than it would be in these days, but, in addition, these were gay young people who rushed about on bicycles or on foot, shouting after and teasing each other. At home, after dark, they ate their evening meal in a lighted room without lowering the blinds, people said in shocked voices you could see all over the room and what was on the table. They had one of the new phonographs, the first to be seen or heard in those parts, and on warm summer evenings they would take this out on the lawn in front of their house and dance to its raucous strains. That was about all that was known about them, excepting that the women smoked cigarettes and were suspected of powdering their faces, but it was sufficient to focus the attention of the scandalmongers and soon it was whispered around that they were living in sin. Which probably they were, for who is entirely guiltless? But they were not living in sin in the restricted sense implied by the gossips for, as after events proved, the young women were sisters and each of them legally married to one of their male companions.

There were others, too, who from time to time were known as "that Bohemian lot up at so-and-so," once a middle-aged couple who had a young girl living with them. Then it was said that the girl was the man's mistress and that his wife knew of and condoned this. Actually she was his ward and his and his wife's adopted daughter. The whole story had arisen out of the fact that she had a different name to theirs and, the wife being a semi-invalid, and much indoors, the girl was the man's constant companion on walks and bicycle rides.

• • •

... disbelieving nine tenths of what she heard and regarding the other one tenth with suspicion. All she really knew about them was through the telegrams they sent and received and some of these were certainly revealing, though not more so than others sent and received by members of strictly conventional families. But married or living in sin, bankrupt or solvent, possessed of but the one set of clothes in which they stood upright or of a full wardrobe, she liked what she saw of the local Bohemians. Their warm, human manner, ready wit, and disdain for convention appealed to her, and she liked their free, careless, artistic style of dress, the men's shabby flannels or tweeds and open shirt collars and the women's bright colours and picturesque hats which looked well on them though they would not have suited their critics. And, after all, it turned out that both couples were married, though they may have been married at a registry office, as some people said, and they were in no danger of bankruptcy, only a little careless of money matters, which left no other grounds for their reputation but their style of dress and the fact that they shared a house which was less usual in those than in these days.

෴෴෴

110

6. The 'lost chapter' of Heatherley—'The Jeromes'

"Bohemia" was a word on everybody's lips in those days. Like the old lady's Mesopotamia it was "a blessed word" which had a fine, sophisticated sound and could mean a great deal, or very little. An impromptu picnic, informal manners, an easy, careless style of dress, especially if it included big, loose bows, or bright colours, a friendship between two of opposite sexes, all passed as Bohemian with many who knew nothing of that country or its sea-coast. Others, and those of the kind not to be trifled with, classed as Bohemian those they suspected of loose morals, of not paying their debts, or of being incompetent housekeepers. It could be applied to a girl who had appeared in public with a little powder on her nose, to a woman who, having a maid, opened the front door herself to visitors, or to a couple who were living together without marriage, or who starved their servants and beat their children. Any departure from convention, short of punishable crime was Bohemian.

There were at and around Heatherley several families of Bohemian repute, but with these Laura's contacts were but slight. Excepting in the matter of being privy to the contents of the telegrams they sent and received, some of those were certainly revealing, though not much more so than some others sent and received by strictly conventional families. In the days before the telephone was in general use, it was nothing out of the ordinary for an operator to handle a telegram of a hundred or more words in length and of the nature of a private letter. People in love with each other and therefore regardless of expense ~~did a good deal in this way to swell the revenue~~ were in this way good customers of the Post Office Department.

Laura's introduction to Bohemia came about in this ~~way~~ manner. She had for some time noticed with interest, and always on a Saturday, a rather peculiar looking couple at the post office counter. The husband was a large, tall man, past the prime of life, decidedly aristocratic looking, and with a voice and accent closely resembling that of elderly Victorian gentlemen in BBC broadcast plays. It was, as a matter of fact, the only instance in which Laura heard anything approaching that accent and intonation in real life. Perhaps she had been born too late, or it may be that they were not as general as is now supposed. Mr

Jerome wore in summer a black alpaca jacket and a limp white Panama hat and often carried a large flag basket, such as workmen used at that time.

Mrs Jerome was a complete contrast to her husband. She was much younger, small, and what was then called "dressy", and her English, though that of an educated woman, had a slight Cockney accent. She had been pretty in her youth and her features were still good, but, as such small, fair women so often do, she had worn badly. At forty, her complexion had faded, the skin of her neck had shrivelled, and the hair, which an artist had remarked when he painted it resembled sunshine, by that time was the colour of string. Yet she had the air of knowing herself to be an attractive woman, and she was an attractive woman. ~~One had only to be on intimate terms with her~~ ... She had *chic*, wit and charm.

She was of French birth, though born and brought up in London, where her father had acted as official interpreter at a large railway terminus. And, all her life, she dressed the part of a Frenchwoman, favouring black for outdoor wear, with small, natty little hats, usually of her own concoction.

A loose quill in Mrs Jerome's hat—toque was the proper name for such hats when in fashion—introduced Laura to the couple. She asked for a pin, and, as it was a very quiet time, with no one but themselves in the office, and Laura had a needle and cotton handy, she offered to stitch it in for her. After that had been done, but not by Laura, for Mrs Jerome had seized the needle and had the quill set at the smartest possible angle in a trice, they remained chatting pleasantly for a few minutes, as people will do who feel themselves under some small obligation.

After that, they became more friendly at each visit, and, early in their acquaintanceship, Laura learned that Mrs Jerome was schoolmistress in a neighbouring village. On Saturdays, the school holiday, they combined the pleasant walk between there and Heatherley with the transaction of their post office business, which, though it appeared ordinary to Laura, consisting mostly of buying stamps and posting letters, was, she was told, of too private a nature to be trusted to their own village postmistress. This seeming mystery was a mild one. Mr Jerome was a writer of short stories, and, until he became more successful than he had been up to that time, preferred that his ambition should not be known locally. Of course, as he remarked, there were the returned manuscripts, which "that demned, inquisitive old harridan" was bound to handle, but they might pass with her for wills, or bills, or the County Court summonses, as long as she did not see the addresses of those he sent away. It was a good thing that poor, innocent old Mrs Garbitt could not hear what he said about her, which, however, was said with the highest good humour and all in the way of business—or what he called local colour, for Laura found afterwards that the inquisitive, gossiping old village postmistress was a stock figure in his stories of country life.

At their second or third visit after the quill incident, Laura was invited to tea with them on the next Sunday and soon she was told to come every Sunday, to come after the office closed in the morning and stay the whole day. During her last months at Heatherley she did spend some part of almost every Sunday there and would sometimes walk over on weekday evenings after the office was closed, and she might have gone even more frequently, for she found their company most fascinating, had not Mr Jerome felt it necessary when dusk had fallen to escort her home to the very door. That was due to his old-fashioned, punctilious code of manners. That a young lady should never be allowed out after dark without a male escort, that no lady of any age should open a room door for herself when a man or boy were in the room, that a man in saluting a lady should not merely raise his hat, but totally remove it in a sweeping bow, were canons either inherited, or so firmly engraved on his mind in his youth, that they were held sacred long after he had thrown off what he called the shackles of convention, including conventional religion and politics.

In religion he called himself an agnostic, in politics he tended to what would now be called the extreme Left. In literature alone he was a traditionalist, loving all that is best of past ages, yet, even in that, there was a twist that saddened Laura, for, although he knew what was best and could appreciate it, he aimed in his own writing at little above the lowest.

Reading aloud to the ladies while they did needlework was a special feature of family life as Mr Jerome had known it in his boyhood and when, after his long wanderings, he returned to home life, he was more than willing to revive the old custom. Some part of every Sunday when Laura was with them he read aloud. At first from such writers as Dickens, Thackeray and

Thomas Hardy. He read well, though with some Victorian mannerisms, and he loved and admired the work of all the great writers, but even nearer to his heart was his own latest effort and when Laura had been tested and found worthy he would with many a modest ha and hum and clearing of the throat, read whatever he had written since she had last been there.

Then Laura was in a delicate position. She was proud to be trusted and liked to see him so happy and hopeful, but admire his writing she could not. It struck her and always struck her as a queer freak of human nature that one who knew and could appreciate all that was best in literature should fall to such a low level in his own writing. Not that that was unusual in real life, she often afterwards applied Meredith's lines "All the oceans tramp and roar to throw that faint white line upon the shore" to the best she herself could do after a lifetime spent in studying the best models; but at that time she had never before been on intimate terms with a writer, good, bad or indifferent, and she had an idea that according to a man's reading, so he would write.

Mr Jerome aimed, as he said, at writing a good magazine story, but his work was not favoured by magazine editors and only very occasionally by the editors of small penny weeklies.

Mr Jerome was fond of talking about plots. A plot, he said, must be worked out architecturally, and to aid him in this he had invented a system of graphs. Then every character must be true to type. He was very firm on that point. And local colour must be added to put flesh upon what he called the skeleton. The system sounded most impressive to Laura, and her disappointment was great when story after story he had written proved to be nothing more than a caricature of the most ordinary type of popular fiction. His hero and heroine had names, but needed them not, for they might just as well have been labelled hero and heroine; his guardian, for there was usually a guardian, who was so shifty in expression that the reader knew at once that he had appropriated the fortune of his ward, unless he happened to be the type of guardian who was destined to marry his ward, when he was younger, handsome and self-sacrificing. What he called his local colour consisted of the throwing in free, gratis and for nothing, of a few rustics speaking an unidentified dialect.

It was with mixed feelings that Laura heard from Mrs Jerome that her husband had put her in one of his stories. It was a great honour, of course, and a compliment, for she felt she could not be as uninteresting as she had thought if a story could be written about her, even one of Mr Jerome's stories. On the other hand, supposing it were published, and a few of his stories were published, what would people who knew her think when they read it. She need not have been afraid. When the story was read out by Mr Jerome, his eyes as often on her face as on his manuscript to ascertain the impression it made upon her, its heroine proved indeed to have the same colour eyes, hair and complexion as herself, but there the resemblance ended and she was soon free to enjoy the idea of herself in a white silk ball dress with a spray of pink roses on the shoulder. As she went to bed that night, feeling a little discontented because in real life she had never been to a ball or had an evening dress of any kind and was never likely to have one, she stood still suddenly while putting her nightdress over her head and said, "A fat lot he knows about me or any other girl!" Though poorly expressed, her saying was true. He knew no more than the outside appearance of her or anyone, perhaps not even excepting his wife, for one human being may adore another without the least understanding of their inner nature. A cynic might say that the less understanding the greater the adoration, and perhaps it is better for most people not to peer too closely into human nature and its motives, but a born writer has no need to peer, he sees by the light of his own nature.

Mr Jerome, then, was not a born writer, or, indeed a good, or a successful writer, but his writing had brought him into touch with writing men, chiefly journalists, and as often one or other of these ran down from town on a Sunday to see him, Laura had the advantage of hearing their conversation. By that time she had been promoted to pouring out at the tea table, Alicia preferring to lie back in her easy chair with her teacup balanced upon the arm, ~~waving her cigarette in the air as she joined in the conversation~~ while she puffed at her cigarette with a detached, yet faintly amused expression. The men would sit at the table for an hour, talking shop, as they called it, and Laura would not have missed a word of this talk for worlds. It is not to be supposed that Gustavious Salisbury, Mr Pennington-White or any of the others with equally impressive names were at then top of their profession, but to Laura at that time they were accepted as being so, and when "the Street" or the office of such-and-such a periodical were mentioned casually, she was puffed up with pride at the thought that at last she was moving in literary circles. Sometimes one of them would take away with him one of Mr Jerome's short stories which all present had agreed needed only a personal introduction to immediately be accepted by an editor, and although this happened time after time with no result, a few weeks of hopeful expectation followed. Mrs Jerome once told Laura that at such times Mr Jerome would stand inside the front door watching the letter box for half an hour before the postman could possibly arrive, his nerves on edge and his attitude tense with anxiety, which manifestation she attributed to his artistic temperament. The usual outcome was that, after weeks of suspense, the manuscript was returned by the friend who had volunteered to negotiate, or the friend might forget to return and, when a pressing invitation to come down for a Sunday put him in mind of it, he would bring it back in his pocket. Laura often wondered if Alicia had the great faith she professed in her husband's future as a writer ~~and when she saw~~ *[page or pages missing?]* ....

• • •

There was no official schoolhouse and their home was one of a row of small detached modern cottages. Laura afterwards declared that on her first visit she would have known the house to be theirs by its outside appearance. All the other houses in the row had stiff white lace curtains, tied back, but not too far back lest the neighbours look in, with broad ribbon sashes while the windows at Number Nine had plain dark green curtains, pulled well back. The Jeromes used the best, front downstairs room as a living room and took their meals there, often at summer suppertime with the curtains undrawn after the lamp was lighted, liking, as they said, to see the night sky and breath the fresh air. This habit of theirs, together with others, such as Mrs Jerome's occasional cigarette, and their way of walking out into the fields together with no hats on, rather scandalized their near neighbours. But they were very well liked in the village, for Mrs Jerome was well esteemed as a teacher who had her pupils well in hand, and, as to Mr Jerome, anybody could see that he was a gentleman born. Though how they came to get married at their time of life, and her with a good salary and home of her own, puzzled most of the villagers. Some were inclined to think that Mr Jerome had married for a home and was living on his wife's earnings, but, against that, she spent money more freely in the matter of charring and laundry than formerly. Surely, they said, if she'd just taken him in as a kindness, he'd have done the housework himself while she was at school, instead of just doing the garden and all that letter-writing. There he sat, at that writing-desk right slap in front of the window, hour after hour, writing away for dear life, anybody might go and look right in the window and he wouldn't know or take any notice. Peculiar, that was what they were, a bit peculiar, which being translated became Bohemian.

Their living room delighted Laura, for as well as what she thought fine paintings on the walls, there were various curios Mr Jerome had collected on his travels and books everywhere. A well-filled bookcase reached to the ceiling and an overflow of books on tables and chairs, and even on the floor in one corner. These last she was told were waiting for new shelves to be fixed in a recess by the fireplace, but they were still piled in the corner nine months later, when Laura left Heatherley. The other rooms were similarly crowded with the contents of the packing cases Mr Jerome had brought to an already well-filled house. But the Jeromes lived cheerfully in spite of the disorder, and very comfortably. Laura opened her eyes widely on one chilly summer evening when one of them proposed a fire should be lighted and the other put a match to the one already laid in the grate. When, thinking it had been lighted at least partly for her own comfort, she remarked that it seemed a pity to soil the grate, Alicia, for she was Alicia to Laura by that time, laughed and said carelessly, "Mrs Brown will have to clear the mess up. She doesn't come tomorrow for it is her washing day, but she'll be here on Tuesday morning, and we can stand the emu feather screen in front of the grate to hide the ashes." Another habit which in Laura's eyes marked Alicia as Bohemian was sewing on Sunday. She had always something of her own to repair or bring up to date. When ruching had gone out and tucks were in fashion she would spend a whole Sunday unpicking and pressing and stitching the front of one of her blouses. Then she had her almost weekly millinery bout. Her talent in this line almost amounted to magic. She would take a few square inches of velvet, ruffle, stitch, pat and pull it, stick a quill at one side, or drape it with a veil, then, holding it at arms length, say, "How do you like my new toque?" "Three guineas at Heath's," her husband would say promptly, and, at least to Laura's unsophisticated eyes it did look much the same as those small, expensive hats from the best shops which were known as creations. Her husband took great pride in his wife's dress. "Trust a Frenchwoman's taste!" he would say to Laura; but what Laura thought the most endearing feature in them both was the great zest and enjoyment they extracted from everything.

It was an exciting experience to her to sit at a tea-table where the master of the house drank unsweetened tea from a glass, with a slice of lemon floating on the surface and, after tea, the lady of the house smoked cigarettes, and, more exciting still to listen to their talk at table. Mrs Jerome so vivacious and witty, with a keen edge to her wit which amounted at times to malice, and her husband, more humorous than witty, telling some story of his youth in London, or of some adventure he had had on his travels. He belonged to a family of artists. His brother, he said, had been praised as a colourist by Ruskin, and only his early death had prevented his rising to fame. Though not a painter himself, Mr Jerome had known Burne-Jones, Watts and Rossetti, and others whose names were by that time well known in art and literature. He said he had himself been the bad boy of the family and, excepting for a few years as a medical student, had settled to no profession. While still a very young man he had joined in the rush for the Australian gold fields, raising no gold, but, as he expressed it, digging hard for experience. After that, he had become a prospector for metals in South Africa, a tea planter in India, finally, he had turned trader and in that way made enough of a fortune to enable him to return and live in a modest way in his native country.

Then he and his wife were deeply in love with each other. Laura had had no idea before that middle-aged people could be in love, but these were, she was sure of that, not only because they made no secret of it, but by the way they looked at and spoke to each other. At first she was a little shocked that it should be so, for it was contrary to all she had learned from the novelists. Love, according to them, was the prerogative of the young and fair, or at least the interesting-looking, excepting of course Esmond and his Lady Castlewood, but when she heard the Jerome's love story, she found it as exciting as any novel.

One day, when she had known her for some time, Alicia took off a thin gold ring, set with a garnet, which she wore above her wedding ring and pointed to her own name engraved inside it, "Alicia." That, she said, was my engagement ring, but it was not a new one, when the name was engraved, I was just a month old. Then she told Laura that, on the day she was born, her mother was taken ill prematurely. She was out at the time, but managed to get home unaided and say to their one small servant: "Call somebody," and the maid, in a great fright, rushed to the door and begged a lady who happened to be passing if she would come to her mistress. The lady, although a stranger, came in ~~and took charge of the case~~, got the patient to bed and summoned doctor and nurse and remained in the house until Alicia was born. After that, the elder Mrs Jerome and Alicia's mother became close friends.

That lady was Mr Jerome's mother, he being then a youth of eighteen. Naturally, when the time for christening the baby came, she was asked to be little Alicia's godmother, and, on that occasion, Alicia's father, in what his daughter when telling the story called "his graceful French way," presented the ring engraved with the baby's name, Alicia, as a small token of his gratitude.

From that time a close friendship existed between the two families. The Jeromes were much better-off and lived in a larger and more comfortable house than the Denairs, and the elder Jeromes were much older than Alicia's parents, but otherwise they had much in common, both couples being lively happy-go-lucky people with little regard for convention, surrounded in their respective streets with neighbours of the heavily respectable Victorian type. By the time little Alicia could toddle she felt herself as much at home in her "Auntie" Jerome's house as she did in that of her parents. The Jerome's house had a garden, the Denair's had none, and when Mrs Jerome knew that her friend was especially busy, or when it was a finer day than usual, Alicia would be fetched by herself or one of her boys to play on the lawn beneath the apple tree there. Wilmot, who did much of his studying at home, was the one usually sent to fetch her. He often went on his own initiative, for he was remarkably fond of the little girl, so much so, that his devotion to her became a family joke in both families. He would lie at full length on his back on the grass and hold her above him at arm's length, carry her pick-a-back round the garden, or play at bears or lions with her among the gooseberry bushes. He said himself in after years that when he once had been left in charge of her and she appeared to be uncomfortable he had changed her napkin. That may have been said to tease his wife, but it was at least certain that he as a nearly grown-up young man had shown an extraordinary interest in and love of little Alicia. And, family tradition added, she had been so fond of her Motand, as she called him, that often when he had taken her home and turned to go she had stretched out her arms and cried.

She had been too young at that time to remember all that, for, before she was two years old, Wilmot Jerome had abandoned his medical studies and left home, without permission being asked or granted, to join in the rush for the Australian gold fields. According to his own account, he raised no gold, though his hard labour brought him a rich haul of experiences. He was next heard of by his family prospecting for metals in South Africa, then as tutor to the sons of a diamond merchant on the Rand, and, finally, as a trader at Beira. The Denair family heard nothing further of his adventurous life, for, by that time, both Mr and Mrs Jerome had died and their only son living in England had married and gone from the district.

By the time she had reached the age of thirty, Alicia was also an orphan. She had taken up teaching and, after her time at a Training College, had left London for Yorkshire where she remained for many years. She loved the North of England people for their sincerity and outrightness of speech. "No humbug about *them*," she would say when speaking about them, but, strangely for one so communicative in general, that was almost all Laura ever heard her say about her long sojourn among them. Excepting that she had three times been engaged to be married and once come very near to the day of the intended ceremony, but she had, as she expressed it, always thought better of it before the actual knot was tied. So there were long blank, or semi-blank spaces in the life story of both husband and wife as known to Laura.

Three years before Laura knew her she had come south, to escape, she said, from her last marriage engagement, and taken up her then present post in a Hampshire village. She had settled down, as she thought, to perpetual spinsterhood, busy and happy in her work, with her hobby of dress to amuse her spare hours, and her pension to look forward to, her only regret being caused by the total absence of anyone with her own tastes or temperament with whom to associate, when Wilmot Jerome re-appeared.

He had returned to England, hoping to spend the rest of his life there, not with a fortune, far from it, but with sufficient means to maintain an old bachelor in modest comfort and, finding she was the only survivor of those he had left light-heartedly and without a farewell as a young man, he had determined to track down Alicia. He managed, after some trouble, to do this, and came down to Hampshire to see her, thinking only to stay a day or [two] and talk over old times, but he stayed on, week after week, at the small inn where he had put up, supposedly for the fishing, and, before the summer ended they had been secretly married one Saturday morning in the nearest large town. Their marriage was a secret one and was, for some time kept secret, because at that time, under the authorities she was subject to, a woman teacher was expected to resign her appointment upon marriage. She had no wish to give up her work or the prospect of the pension due to her in a few years.

Although her husband had sufficient means to keep them both comfortably in a small way, after her independent life, she said, she would hate to be dependant upon another, especially upon the man she loved so passionately. Love should be a gift, she told Laura, not a matter of work and wages. And when Laura, who knew quite well that that marriage meant more than that, said, "Marriage is often work without wages," she said that was worse still. The secret of their marriage was soon out, however, a man whether a stranger or locally-known cannot be seen visiting the home of a village schoolmistress at all hours without causing scandal. The clergyman, who was one of the school managers, interviewed Alicia and had to be told of the marriage. He, personally, was against the compulsory retirement of married school teachers and promised to use his influence with the county authorities to make an exception in her case. Meanwhile Alicia continued her teaching and her husband came to live at her house, and no decision as to her retirement was reached during the time Laura knew the Jeromes.

᷇᷇᷇᷇᷇

Tree roots form a wall along a typical 'sunken lane' near Bramshott

Flora's Trail

ଚ୍ଚ ଚ୍ଚ ଚ୍ଚ

— a guided walk —
from
Grayshott to Griggs Green
[Heatherley to Peverel]
and back again

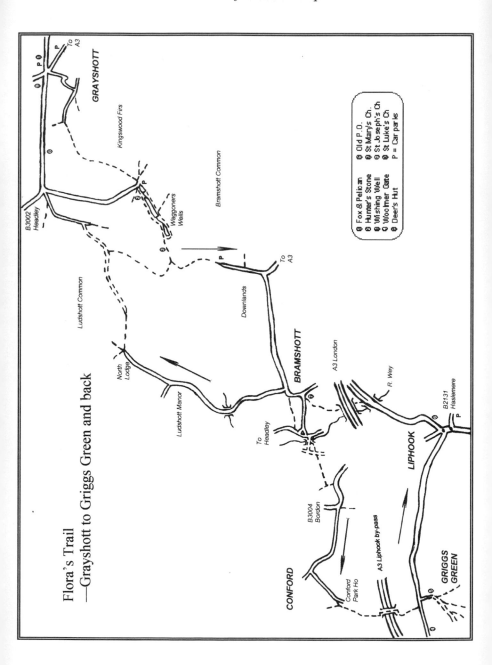

Flora's Trail
—Grayshott to Griggs Green and back

GRAYSHOTT

Kingswood Firs

B3002
Headley

Bramshott Common

Ludshott Common

North Lodge

Ludshott Manor

Waggoners Wells

To A3

Downlands

BRAMSHOTT

A3 London

R. Wey

LIPHOOK

B2131
Haslemere

To Headley

B3004
Bordon

CONFORD

Conford Park Ho

A3 Liphook by-pass

GRIGGS GREEN

Fox & Pelican
Hunter's Stone
Wishing Well
Woolmer Gate
Deer's Hut

Old P.O.
St Mary's Ch.
St Joseph's Ch.
St Luke's Ch
P = Car parks

Grayshott to Griggs Green and back

Distance approximately 5 miles there and 5 miles back (allow about 2 hours each way)

᠗᠑ ᠗᠑ ᠗᠑

Much of the outward route, starting at the *Fox and Pelican* in Grayshott, and ending at the *Deers Hut* in Griggs Green, is little changed from the time Flora herself might have walked it—and both these hostelries are ones which she would have known.

From the *Fox and Pelican*, turn right for about 50 yards to the 'Fiveways' crossroads.

[To visit the site of Flora's post office, cross over and walk along the right of Crossways Road for about a hundred yards, past the present post office to the property called *Pendarvis House*. The original building here was demolished in 1986.]

From 'Fiveways,' take the unsurfaced Hill Road, said to be named after broomsquire William 'Body' Hill who lived here in Flora's time. The garden behind the hedge on the right belongs to *Apley House*, built for Edgar Leuchars in 1880. He was the man who pressed for a telegraph service to be installed at Grayshott post office in 1890.

At the end, turn right down Stoney Bottom. This is the nearest of the 'escape routes' which Flora could have used when leaving the post office for a walk in the surrounding countryside. In May 1900, a Dr Coleclough was caught and prosecuted for trying to poison the dog of James Belton, who lived down here—an incident which Flora recalls at some length in *Heatherley*.

Fork right at the bottom, and proceed down the valley track, which leads towards Waggoners Wells. In a while, note the houses up on the hill to the right. One of these used to be called *Mount Cottage*, and in the late 1870s was a small village shop run by Henry Robinson. It was bought by Mr I'Anson (see below), and Mr Robinson moved to Crossways Road to build a shop there which became the first post office in 1887. [At the time of writing, Grayshott Post Office has returned to this original building, although now situated at the other end of it.]

125

After passing a track which comes steeply down from the right, look for the buildings of the *Cenacle* convent among the trees in the same direction—it has a small cross on the top of one of its eaves. This is the site of Edward I'Anson's first house in Grayshott, built on enclosed common land in 1862 and originally named *Heather Lodge*. Family tradition says he rode on horseback from Clapham to view the plot prior to the purchase.

In those days, Grayshott was noted as a lawless area in which gangs of robbers roamed freely, and I'Anson was warned that they would never allow a stranger to settle among them. But he persevered, and he and his family not only lived peaceably, but also began exercise a 'benevolent aristocracy' over the other inhabitants of the growing village, his daughter Catherine becoming particularly active on the parish council and other local organising bodies.

Up on the opposite side of the valley, invisible among the trees, is a house now called *Hunter's Moon*, but originally named *Kingswood Firs*. It was built in 1887 by James Mowatt who was, in a way, instrumental in Flora leaving Grayshott, since it was he who pressed for a rival telegraph service to be established in Hindhead.

Keep to the valley path, past a pumping station, and through the wooden barrier. In a while the track moves from the valley floor where this becomes overgrown and boggy, and you pass a series of small ponds before arriving at the top lake of Waggoners Wells.

Before the days of the motor car, the road which crosses the stream here was used as a route for traffic between Haslemere and Frensham. Cross the ford by the footbridge and then turn left to follow the path along the right-hand bank of the lake.

Note shortly the stone dedicated to Sir Robert Hunter, a founder of The National Trust in 1895, who lived in Haslemere and was also employed by the post office, though in a somewhat more senior position than Flora—he was legal advisor at Head Office. Flora would have been aware of a well-reported battle taking place during her time in Grayshott, to protect Hindhead Common. Sir Robert was involved in this, and a few years later initiated a local 'buy-out' to transfer it to the Trust. After his death, Waggoners Wells was also acquired by the Trust, and was dedicated to his memory in 1919. [Note the unusual spelling of 'Waggeners' on it—originally the ponds were called 'Wakeners Wells']

Flora says she 'did not often linger by the lakes' on her Sunday walks, but 'climbed at once by a little sandy track to the heath beyond.' To your right there are several tracks leading uphill to Ludshott Common, and perhaps she met old 'Bob Pikesley' up there or on one of the other local commons, herding his three or four cows.

Also in that direction is Grayshott Hall, site of the old Grayshott Farm rented for several months in 1867 by Alfred Tennyson and his family while building a house of their own near Haslemere. It is said that he wrote his short ode 'Flower in the crannied wall' while he was here, some thirty years before Flora trod the same paths.

Cross the dam of the top pond, and continue down the left-hand bank of the second pond. Here in autumn, the colour of the trees opposite reflected in the water still brings photographers to the site, as it did in Flora's time.

The ponds are not natural, having been built in the first half of the 17th century by Henry Hooke, lord of the manor of Bramshott and a local ironmaster. He already had ironworks in the neighbouring Hammer Vale, and presumably wanted to add to his capacity by building another works here. But he seems not to have done so—or at least no evidence of an ironworks has ever been found—and we are left instead to enjoy these quiet pools as his legacy. Flora's husband John used to come fishing here when they lived at Liphook.

The walk may be continued down either side of the third pond, although the path on the left bank is easier. Note the small quarry in the right bank by each dam. It was from here that material was taken to build them, over 300 years ago.

At the dam to the third (and last) pond, take the right-hand side again, and follow the path past *Summerden* to the wishing well. When Flora first saw this she described it as 'a deep sandy basin fed by a spring of crystal clear water which gushed from the bank above' and said that it had dozens of pins at the bottom which had been dropped in it for luck—some by her. However when she returned in the 1920s, *Summerden* had been built and the water then 'fell in a thin trickle from a lead pipe, the sandy basin having been filled in.' People, she said, seemed to have forgotten its existence.

She might be happier today to see it has not quite been forgotten. Although there is no longer a sandy basin, a new well now invites the passer-by to throw in a coin for the benefit of The National Trust—and, of course, to make a wish.

Carry on down the path, cross the stream by the footbridge, and follow the bridle path to the right and up a sunken track. (In muddy conditions you may wish to take the alternative but steeper route on higher ground). At the crest of the hill keep following this track down and then steeply up the other side of a valley, with the fence of Downlands Estate to your right. In about half a mile, after passing an area used as a car park, the track becomes a paved road.

To your left is Bramshott Common and the site of Ontario Camp, one of several encampments built in the district by Canadian soldiers during the Second World War. The common had been used extensively by Canadians in the First World War also, and Flora mentions in one of her *Peverel Papers* how 'row upon row of wooden huts, churches, shops and theatres sprang up in a week or two. The whole place became a populous town.' That site is now commemorated by a double row of maple trees along the sides of the A3 Portsmouth road.

To your right is *Downlands*, which attracted riders such as Princess Anne to the Horse Trials held here annually from 1963 until 1982.

After about half a mile, turn right down another paved road (Rectory Lane) and past the main entrance to *Downlands*. The road soon becomes one of the typical 'sunken lanes' of the region before emerging in Bramshott village.

Where the paved road bears left, continue through some railings and down the sunken path ahead. Here you can imagine more easily how many of the local lanes would have looked in earlier times *(see photo p.122)*. At the bottom, turn left and past a terrace of houses on the right—a shop and post office were here in Flora's day. Note also on your left the house aptly named *Roundabout*, wedged between the forks of the road coming down from Bramshott church. This was once the home of actor Boris Karloff.

Continue along the road ahead for a few yards, then right at the gate to *Bramshott Vale* and up the track which passes over the headwaters of the southern River Wey. Shortly afterwards, go left through a kissing gate, cut across a field and over two stiles towards an avenue of lime trees.

Don't be alarmed at this point to find yourself in the company of some very docile highland cattle. These and other animals are used in season as part of a natural heathland management scheme for local commons, cropping vegetation such as birch, gorse and grass, and allowing the heather to flourish. One feels that Flora would have approved.

Follow footpath signs diagonally across the avenue, through a small metal gate, across a farmyard, over a stile by a larger metal gate and then follow a path along the right-hand side of a field. Turn left at a T-junction of paths and over a stile to meet the B3004 Liphook to Bordon road.

Cross carefully and turn right, going along the pavement for about a hundred yards to where the road bears sharp right. Follow the bridleway sign straight ahead down the drive towards *Conford Park House*. After slightly more than half a mile, bear left at a grass triangle, cross a bridge by a weir, and pass through some iron gates. Take the footpath to the right, immediately after the gatehouse garden, following behind the line of a hedge. Pass through a smaller iron gate, cross a clearing in front of an old cottage and take the footpath signposted straight ahead. This soon joins a bridleway and winds generally uphill through a beech wood. It can be rather muddy in places.

Bear left just before a gate to an Army firing range, and follow Bridleway signs across a new bridge over the by-pass (which now takes the London to Portsmouth traffic away from the centre of Liphook), and eventually down to meet Longmoor Road. In earlier days the road led out onto Woolmer Forest and ended; later it became a through road to the army camp at Longmoor; today it is the spur to an intersection on the new A3.

The house called *Woolmer Gate*, to which Flora and her family moved in 1926, is just along the road to the right—but to arrive at the *Deers Hut*, cross the road and go up the drive almost opposite towards a small cluster of cottages—the original hamlet of Griggs Green. In her 1925 *Guide to Liphook*, Flora says 'it was one of the old forest ale-houses, nor has its function altered much, for neighbours from the scattered houses upon the heath still meet there upon summer evenings to take a glass and discuss things ... just as their forbears must have done for centuries.'

Tracks, once more frequently used, lead from Griggs Green southwards to Forest Mere and beyond, and upwards onto Weaver's Down. This is Flora's *Peverel*—'a land of warm sands, of pine and heather and low-lying bog-lands.' She urges you to 'take one of the multitudinous pathways at pleasure; each one leads sooner or later to the summit from which, on a clear day, magnificent views reward the climber. Forest Mere lake lies like a mirror in the woods directly beneath; to the south is the blue ridge of the South Downs; to the north the heathery heights of Hindhead.'

At the end of this section of the guide, Flora adds enigmatically: 'It does not come within the scope of the present work to dwell upon the beauty and interest of this spot more fully; the present writer hopes to deal more fully with it in a future book.' As far as we know, that book never materialised.

Return to Grayshott

Distance approximately 5 miles (allow about 2 hours)

೧ೀ ೧ೀ ೧ೀ

There is a lack of convenient public transport between Liphook and Grayshott. For those wishing to make the return journey to Grayshott by foot, here is an alternative which forms a 'figure of eight' with the route out, crossing it at Bramshott.

From the *Deers Hut*, turn right along Longmoor Road for the mile-long walk towards the centre of Liphook. John Thompson and Diana would have cycled to work by this route after they moved to Griggs Green. Along this road also there were one or two small private schools, and Peter Thompson may well have attended one of them. On page 12 of the 1925 *Guide to Liphook*, for example, Miss A. B. Skevington advertises her 'Day School for Girls and Preparatory School for Boys' in a house called *Woodheath*.

At the Square take the second road left (London Road) which, before the village was by-passed, bore all the road traffic between Portsmouth and London. On the right-hand side of the road, note the Midland Bank, which was the post office when Flora was here. There is a plaque on the house to its left, where she lived with her family from 1916 to 1926.

Further along the road on the right is the old school building now used as a public library. If it is open, you may care to go inside and inspect the sculpture of Flora by Philip Jackson, commissioned in 1981 and moved to the library in 1995.

Follow the left-hand side of London Road out of the village and over the river, following the old road to the left where it divides from the new. Note to the left of the road bridge an old aqueduct over the river, part of a large network of irrigation sluices and channels which stretched for miles along the valley. These were designed to obtain a second annual harvest of animal fodder by flooding the riverside meadows at intervals, and are now part of a conservation project.

About fifty yards after crossing the river, take the footpath to the left. This leads into the back of Bramshott churchyard, and was used in Flora's day by Liphook schoolboys attending Bramshott school—the Liphook school being only for girls. In her *Guide to Liphook*, Flora said: 'The raised footpath over-hangs, like a terrace, the valley of the infant Wey, a small streamlet at this point, but already known locally as "The River." The path is, and has been from time immemorial, the approach from this side of the parish to the Parish Church.'

Its peace has been somewhat shattered in recent years by the construction of the large by-pass bridge overhead.

On entering the churchyard, you will see to your left the rows of graves of the Canadian soldiers who died in the military hospital on Bramshott Common during the First World War—many from the influenza epidemic in late 1918 rather than from enemy action. Their Catholic colleagues are laid to rest at St Joseph's church in Grayshott, which you will pass later.

On the other side of the churchyard wall, to your right, note the rear of Bramshott Manor which is said to be one of the oldest continually inhabited houses in Hampshire, dating as it does from the year 1220. Flora said: 'Very few houses of its antiquity have escaped so well the hands of the restorer.'

Continue through the churchyard and turn right towards Bramshott church itself ('only five years younger than the Magna Carta') which is well worth a visit.

Leave the churchyard by the lych gate, cross over the road and proceed straight ahead. Soon you retrace your steps of the outward journey up Rectory Lane for a few yards, then take the road to the left which is signposted Ludshott Manor.

Follow this road, which dips down to cross the stream coming from Waggoners Wells, then rises to run past *Spring Pond Cottage* (a favourite of Flora's) and the entrance to *Ludshott Manor* itself.

Where the metalled road bears left, go straight ahead along an unmade track for another half mile or so. Here, at *North Lodge*, you arrive at the entrance to Ludshott Common, an area of wood and heathland which extends for many hundreds of acres and is now owned by The National Trust.

From this point several routes may be struck at will across the common towards Grayshott. The one detailed below skirts its edge.

Go through the wooden posts, and turn right following the bridleway around the edge of the common. It can be boggy in places, but this improves when the first of two houses is reached and the track becomes a roughly surfaced access road. Continue along this, ignoring turns to the right which lead down to the valley of Waggoners Wells.

In Flora's time, the view to your left would have been open, with purple heather and yellow gorse stretching almost as far as the eye could see. Lack of animal grazing since then has allowed the trees to grow here, but if you walk towards the middle of the common you will find areas which the National Trust has brought back to the original state. And there, as dusk falls on a summer evening, you can still hear the drumming of the Nightjar which so fascinated Tennyson when he lived here.

About half a mile past the houses, you suddenly find yourself on concrete. This is a remnant of Superior Camp, another of the 'Great Lakes' camps built by the Canadians to house their soldiers during the Second World War. The huts were used as temporary accommodation by local civilians for some years afterwards, but now only the footings remain, along with the occasional garden plant looking incongruous in a heathland setting.

Turn left and follow the concrete road to its junction with the B3002 Bordon to Hindhead road. Grayshott House on your right was once the home of the broadcaster Richard Dimbleby.

From here it is a direct walk for about a mile along the pavement and back to Grayshott. In Flora's day this road was described as being 'a sandy track with encroaching gorse!'

St Joseph's, with the Catholic Canadian graves from the First World War, is on your right about fifty yards along the road, next to the driveway to the *Cenacle*.

Further along on the right, note the entrance to *Pinewood*, where the I'Anson family lived for many years. The village school and laundry (now the site of a pottery) along School Lane to the left were both institutions started by them.

St Luke's church, with its impressive spire, is on your left as you arrive back at the village centre. The foundation stone was laid in the summer of 1898 by Miss Catherine I'Anson, shortly before Flora arrived in the village.

At the western end of the churchyard are the graves of Conan Doyle's first wife, Mary, and their son Kingsley who died of wounds in the First World War. And at the eastern end, towards the cross-roads, is that of Harold Oliver Chapman, and his wife Sarah Annie born 29 Sep 1878–died 29 Jun 1969. Perhaps you may care to pause here for a while to remember with affection the 'pretty, blue-eyed, sweet-natured girl of eighteen' who, Flora says, made her life tolerable during her time in Grayshott.

෬ ෬ ෬

And if you feel weary now after your ten miles walk, then reflect as you relax in the *Fox and Pelican* that Flora would have thought nothing of walking nineteen or twenty miles in one of her daily wanderings!

Sculpture of Flora,
now in Liphook library

Other suggested walks from Grayshott

❧ ❧ ❧

Whitmore Vale and Beacon Hill

From the 'Fiveways' crossroads, take Whitmore Vale Road. Follow this downhill and, about a hundred yards after crossing the county boundary, turn up the bridleway going off at right angles to the right.

In about ¼ mile, cross a stream (could this be near Flora's secret 'heart of the wood'?—the area has the right sort of feel), and a fairly stiff uphill walk then brings you to Beacon Hill. Turn right along the main road for about 50 yards to find the village centre. The old post office, to which Annie moved with her husband, was on the corner of Beacon Hill Road.

❧ ❧ ❧

Pollock's Path and Miss James' Walk

From the 'Fiveways' crossroads, take Crossways Road. Follow this downhill past the old county boundary stone, and just after the bottom of the dip take 'Pollock's Path' to the left.

This was named after Sir Frederick Pollock who came to live at *Hindhead Copse* (now part of the *Royal School*) in 1884. He was one of the 'eminent men' who would have been served by Flora in her post office.

Follow the path to its junction with Portsmouth Road, and cross this with care. Continue almost straight ahead, along Hazel Grove. Just before the bend, note *Fir Cottage* on your left. This was the house in which Annie Symonds lived with her parents, and from which she walked into Grayshott each day.

Turn left at the bend along a short track, and enter the National Trust property of 'Miss James' Walk.' This meanders through woodland above Nutcombe Valley, and several alternative paths may be taken from here.

By following the direct path which keeps more or less on the level, you pass behind *West Down* where Miss James and the Bulley family lived, and where Annie's father worked as a gardener. This brings you back out onto the Portsmouth Road near to its junction with Headley Road.

By following paths to the right and downhill, you arrive in the valley which eventually leads up to the rear of *Undershaw*. Turn left up the valley—it is easy to lose your way here and, as the author can testify, find yourself suddenly upon Conan Doyle's back lawn!, but keeping to the main path brings you up and out onto Hindhead Road near to the crossroads. At the corner is the old post office, where the installation of a telegraph machine in August 1900 heralded Flora's departure from Grayshott.

From here you may return to Grayshott by pavement along the Portsmouth and Headley Roads, noting *Undershaw* to your left and the Congregational Hall to your right where Conan Doyle and George Bernard Shaw both spoke at meetings.

Alternatively head for the open expanses of Hindhead Common to visit the cross on Gibbit Hill and the Devil's Punch Bowl. A circuit back to Grayshott is possible by way of Beacon Hill and Whitmore Vale.

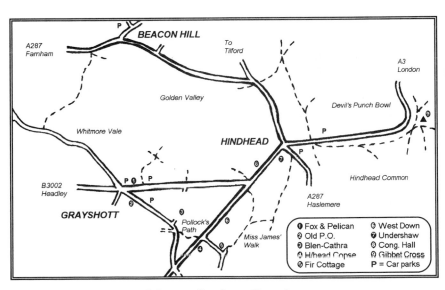

Other walks from Grayshott

Other suggested walks from Liphook

∾ ∾ ∾

Among the many fascinating publications of the Bramshott & Liphook Preservation Society, their *Walks Around Liphook* booklet and *Liphook Walkabout* leaflet can be recommended for those wishing to explore further the countryside of Flora's 'Peverel.' These can be bought in Liphook village, as can a facsimile of the 1925 *Guide to Liphook* mentioned in this book.

There is also a fine set of Literary Walks leaflets produced by East Hampshire District Council, and the *Flora Thompson* walk in this series, prepared by Anne Mallinson, will take you on a guided tour of about six miles around Weavers Down and Holly Hills, starting near the *Deers Hut* public house at Griggs Green.

• • •

The Ordnance Survey Pathfinder map 1266 (Haslemere and Hindhead) covers the walks described in this book.

• • •

Louise Hooker (neé Woods) and Eileen Hobson (neé Leggett) at the unveiling of Flora's sculpture outside the Post Office in Liphook, 1981—sculpture moved inside Library in 1995

Historical Calendar of Events

❧ ❧ ❧

1859 London to Portsmouth Railway opens through Haslemere and Liphook

1861 Edward I'Anson buys Grayshott Park Estate and builds *Heather Lodge*—first new development in Grayshott

1867 Mar: Tennyson rents Grayshott Farm (now Grayshott Hall) for about a year while *Aldworth* is built

1874 Apr 4: John William Thompson born in Ryde, Isle of Wight

1876 **Dec 5: Flora Jane Timms born in Juniper Hill, Oxfordshire *[Lark Rise]***

1878 Flora's brother Edwin Timms born in Juniper Hill
Sep 29: Sarah Annie Symonds *[Alma Stedman]* born in Liscaid, Cheshire

1880 Flora starts attending school at Cottisford, Oxfordshire

1884 Professor John Tyndall builds a house at Hindhead, encouraging other 'eminent men' to follow

1891 Apr: John Thompson begins training in Bournemouth as sorting clerk & telegraphist
Flora begins work at Fringford *[Candleford Green]* post-office, aged 14

1892 Walter Chapman *[Mr Hertford]* takes Grayshott post office
Nov: Annie Symonds moves from Cheshire, aged 13

1896 Arthur Conan Doyle moves to Hindhead for his wife's health

1897 Flora leaves Fringford, (after the Diamond Jubilee celebrations, June 22) to take temporary jobs elsewhere
October: Arthur Conan Doyle moves into *Undershaw*

1898 Flora sees her first moving film in Halstead, Essex
June: George Bernard Shaw (GBS) spends his honeymoon at *Pitfold House*, Hindhead
Jul: Foundation stone laid of St Luke's church, Grayshott

1898 Sept: Flora arrives in Grayshott, aged 21, and lodges with the Chapmans

1898 Nov: Dr Lyndon notes Walter Chapman made accusations of
his wife's immorality at this time
Nov: GBS rents *Blen Cathra* (now St Edmund's School),
Hindhead

1899 Jan 28: GBS delivers a 'vigorous oration' at a Peace Meeting
in Hindhead Congregational Hall — Conan Doyle in the
chair also spoke. Flora mentions attending meetings here
Mar: Flora moves lodgings away from Grayshott post office
August: GBS leaves the district
Aug 23: *Fox & Pelican* opens in Grayshott—Flora orders
her 'immense ninepenny dinners' from it
Flora starts seeing 'Mr Foreshaw' about this time?
Oct 10: Boer War begins
Edwin enlists for Boer War—meets Flora on Aldershot
railway station

1900 Jan 6: Boers attack Ladysmith
May 17: Mafeking relieved
May: Dr Coleclough fined for poisoning dogs at Grayshott
Aug 10: John Volckman *[Mr Foreshaw?]* dies at
Grayshott, aged 63—buried in Headley churchyard
Flora starts seeing 'The Jeromes' about this time?
Sep: Hindhead telegraph facility opens
—earliest date for Flora leaving Grayshott
Oct 17: St Luke's church, Grayshott, consecrated

1901 Jan 22: Queen Victoria dies
May/Jun?: 'Mrs Parkhurst' gives birth to 'Elsie'?
—latest date for Flora leaving Grayshott
Jul 29: Walter Chapman murders his wife Emily at
Grayshott and is committed to Broadmoor

1903 Jan 7: Flora marries John Thompson at St Mary's, Twickenham
Thompsons make home in Winton, a suburb of Bournemouth
Oct 24: Winifred Grace ('Diana') Thompson born in Winton

1906 Mar 15: All five of Walter Chapman's children re-baptised
at St Luke's, Grayshott

1907 Edwin returns from India to work on local farm in Oxfordshire

1909 Early autumn: Flora visits Juniper Hill with Diana to see
     Edwin before he emigrates to Canada
     Oct 6: Henry Basil Thompson born in Winton

1910 Jan 12: Annie Symonds marries Harold Oliver Chapman
     (nephew of Walter) at St Luke's, Grayshott
     Flora's brother Frank Timms goes to Queensland, aged 21

1911 Feb: Flora wins competition in 'The Ladies Companion'
     for essay on Jane Austen
     July: Flora wins again for an essay on Shakespeare's heroines

1912 Short story ('The Toft Cup') published in 'The Ladies
     Companion'—Flora's first payment
     Flora wins prize for writing a crit. on Dr Ronald Macfie's
     ode on the sinking of the *Titanic*
     Macfie visits Flora, and starts a literary correspondence

1913 Flora writes 'The Leper' and sells it to 'The Literary Monthly'

1916 Apr: Flora's brother Edwin killed in action in Belgium
     May 30: Vacancy for postmaster at Liphook advertised
     Aug: Thompson family moves from Bournemouth to Liphook

1917 Flora joins the Haslemere Natural History Society
     (also 1918 & 1922-27) as 'Miss F Thompson'
     Jan: John Mumford arrives in Bramshott—posted to
     France in October

1918 Oct 19: Peter Redmond Thompson born in Liphook
     Nov 11: Armistice day—end of First World War
     Dec: Albert Timms (Flora's father) dies, aged 64

1919 Flora takes a correspondence course in the *Daily News*

1920 Flora writes six stories for 'The Catholic Fireside'

1921 Flora writes 'Out of Doors' nature articles (set in the New
     Forest) for *The Catholic Fireside*
     Book of Flora's poems published: *Bog Myrtle & Peat*—
     her first publicity—pictured at her typewriter and
     reported in the national press
     Country bus services start in Liphook
     ? Flora visited by 'Mrs Parkhurst' from Grayshott
     ? Sep: Flora revisits Grayshott

1922 Flora begins writing her 'Peverel Papers' nature notes (set mainly around Liphook) for *The Catholic Fireside*
Sept: Basil Thompson (aged 12) starts at Churchers College

1923 Peter (aged 5) starts at school

1923-25 Flora writes a 'Fireside Reading Circle' article and a 'Peverel Paper' each month, plus setting and judging competitions and dealing with volumes of correspondence

1924 Flora meets Mildred ('Myldrede') Humble-Smith

1925 Flora helps to write the *Guide to Liphook*
Flora ends the 'Fireside Reading Circle' and starts a postal writers group 'The Peverel Society' with Mildred, issuing 'The Peverel Monthly'

1926 Feb: Basil Thompson (aged 16) and Cecil Cluer (engaged to Diana) go out to Queensland, Australia
Jul 2: Thompsons buy *Woolmer Gate* at Griggs Green

1927 Jul 6: Vacancy for postmaster at Dartmouth advertised
Aug 3: Appointment of John Thompson to Dartmouth recorded in Post Office Circular
Sep 9: *Woolmer Gate* put on the market
Nov 10: Presentation to John Thompson, who moves to Dartmouth—Flora, Diana & Peter stay in Griggs Green
Dec: Last 'Peverel Paper' appears

1928 Flora's novel 'Gates of Eden' appears in serialised form in copies of 'The Peverel Monthly'
Autumn: Flora, Diana & Peter move to Dartmouth

1933 Emma Timms (Flora's mother) dies, aged 80

1935 Apr 12: John Thompson retires

1936 Mar 30: William Elwes *[Richard Brownlow?]* retires from Cable & Wireless
Dec: 'The Lady' magazine publishes Flora's short story 'The Tail-less Fox' (Flora aged 60)

1937 Apr: 'Old Queenie' published in 'The Lady'
Aug: 'An Oxfordshire Hamlet in the Eighties' published in 'The National Review'—becomes the start of 'Lark Rise'
Aug: Basil Thompson marries Dora in America

1938 May: 'May Day in the Eighties' published in 'The
　　　　National Review'
　　　　'Lark Rise' accepted by the Oxford University Press

1939 Mar: 'Lark Rise' published
　　　　Flora starts writing 'Over to Candleford'

1940 Thompsons move to *Lauriston* in Brixham

1941 Feb: Proofs of 'Over to Candleford' ready
　　　　Sep: Peter Thompson lost at sea, aged 22
　　　　'Peverel Society' disbanded

1942 Flora writes 'Candleford Green'

1943 Jan: 'Candleford Green' published

1944 Flora completes 'Heatherley,' but does not submit it

1945 Apr: Trilogy 'Lark Rise to Candleford' published
　　　　Flora starts writing 'Still Glides the Stream'

1946 Aug: Flora completes 'Still Glides the Stream'

1947 Flora writes an article on her life and work for 'Readers News'
　　　　May 21: Flora dies in bed in the evening, aged 70

1948 Jul 13: John Thompson dies, aged 74
　　　　'Still Glides the Stream' published—Diana is literary executor

1957 Margaret Lane's essay published in 'The Cornhill' magazine

1966 Winifred ('Diana') Thompson dies, aged 63
　　　　Flora's papers sent to the University of Texas

1969 Jun 29: Annie Symonds dies, aged 90

1970 Anne Mallinson of Selborne discovers the East Hampshire
　　　　connection with Flora

1976 May: Centenary of Flora's birth—literary lunch held at
　　　　'The Royal Anchor,' Liphook

1978 May: Plaque to Flora unveiled on the old post office at Liphook

1979 'A Country Calendar', an extended biographical essay by
　　　　Margaret Lane, published including 'Heatherley' and
　　　　selections from 'Peverel Papers'
　　　　Plays based on 'Lark Rise' and 'Candleford Green' produced

1981 May 21: Sculptured bust of Flora by Philip Jackson
　　　　unveiled at Liphook, outside the then current post office

1986 More selections from 'Peverel Papers' published
     Building demolished which had housed Grayshott post
     office in Flora's time

1990 Biography of Flora Thompson by Gillian Lindsay published
     Anne Mallinson starts the Selborne Circle of Rural Writers,
     which includes Flora among other local writers

1995 July: Sculpture of Flora moved into the village library at
     Liphook

1997 50th anniversary of Flora's death commemorated
     Play 'Flora's Peverel' performed in East Hampshire

Flora Thompson on Stage

The author of this book has written stage plays covering the two periods of Flora Thompson's life in East Hampshire.

In *Flora's Heatherley* we see her arrive as a young, gauche, country girl and pass, as she says, "from foolish youth to wicked adolescence" in Grayshott. The theme of this play is essentially about the conventions of the late Victorian/early Edwardian period, particularly with respect to courtship and marriage, and Flora's difficulty in conforming to them.

In *Flora's Peverel* we see her fifteen years later, as a married lady with a husband and children of her own. This play brings to life the period in Liphook when, against the odds, she "won the fight to write" as a contemporary of hers put it.

For details and performance rights for both these plays, contact the author at the address shown in this book.

By the same author:—

One Monday in November—the story of the Selborne and Headley Workhouse Riots of 1830

During the 'Swing' riots of 1830, according to the famed historians J.L. & Barbara Hammond, "the most interesting event in the Hampshire rising was the destruction of the workhouses at Selborne and Headley." If these riots had succeeded, "the day when the Headley workhouse was thrown down would be remembered ... as the day of the taking of the Bastille." Here a local historian traces the dramatic events of two days of rioting and its aftermath in the villages and beyond.

ISBN 1-873855-09-5 May 1993 Paperback, A4 landscape, 40pp, illustrations plus maps.

RIOT! or This Bloody Crew—an historical drama

The stage script of the Workhouse Riots story, performed as a community play in October 1993. Includes historical notes.

ISBN 1-873855-01-X November 1993 Paperback, A4 landscape, 36pp, illustrations plus maps.

(Also available on audio cassette as adapted for radio)

All Tanked Up—the Canadians in Headley during World War II

A story of the benign 'invasion' of a Hampshire village by Canadian tank regiments over a period of four years, told from the point of view of both Villagers and Canadians. Includes technical details of tanks, and full Order of Battle for Canadian Regiments in 1945, as well as many personal reminiscences.

ISBN 1-873855-00-1 May 1994 Paperback, A4 landscape, 48pp, illustrations plus maps.

The Sir Robert Hunter Trail, Hindhead Common
—a dramatised two-mile walk

This booklet follows the route of the Sir Robert Hunter Trail on Hindhead Common, inaugurated in the Centenary year of The National Trust. It contains the dramatic material used by the original actors, and also background information relating to the personalities and scenes portrayed. Used by schools and other society groups—the trail is also suitable for wheelchairs.

ISBN 1-873855-13-3 Aug 1995 Paperback, A5 portrait, 24pp, illustrations plus map

By the same author:—

A Balance of Trust—The foundation of The National Trust and 50 years of history in & around Haslemere, 1855-1905

Haslemere was, quite literally, on the road to nowhere until the railway arrived in 1859 and opened up the area as a commuter belt. Ready access to and from London then put pressure on the surrounding common land, giving in-comers incentives to buy and to build. In short, the area was earmarked for invasion.

One such commuter was Sir Robert Hunter, legal adviser to the Post Office, whose vision of the need to secure and protect land of natural beauty for the nation created The National Trust.

From his base in Haslemere we are introduced to events and characters of national significance. Famed for its healthy air, the area soon became the haunt of writers, artists, politicians and scientists of repute. People such as Alfred Lord Tennyson, Helen Allingham and Sir Arthur Conan Doyle were all active in the neighbourhood, and we follow their contribution to the debates of the time. Flora Thompson was there too.

Illustrated throughout with many photographs of the period, it will appeal to those interested in the National Trust, the postal service, great literary characters, 'Green' issues, and the fate of threatened open spaces such as Hindhead Common today.
ISBN 1-873855-12-5 Sep 1995 Paperback, A4 landscape, 60pp, period illustrations plus maps.

By the same publisher:—

Some Ancient Churches in North East Hampshire
—an illustrated collection of notes

Twelve fascinating churches in the north east corner of Hampshire are described. A map on the back cover guides you through the picturesque lanes of the area, and 33 photographs give both exterior and interior views of each church. Villages include Bentley ("The Village" of the TV & Radio series), Selborne of Gilbert White fame, East Worldham with the body of Chaucer's wife, Binsted where Montgomery of Alamein lies, and Bramshott, the final resting place for so many Canadian servicemen of the First World War. A short glossary is included for those unfamiliar with some of the architectural terms used. Suitable size for the pocket.
ISBN 1-873855-11-7 April 1995 Paperback, A5 portrait, 28pp, illustrations plus map.